Foreword

It has been said that the richest plots of land in the world aren't the diamond mines in South Africa, nor the oil fields in the Middle East, but rather the graveyards and cemeteries because that's where people and their dreams are buried. There are life-changing and world-changing people and ideas which will never be heard because they never had the chance to reach the masses.

Using their life experiences, these authors have proven that if you have a willingness to do whatever is required, and take the initiative to pursue your dreams, you can make some incredible things happen.

If you are willing to elevate your life beyond your circumstances and allow that to become your life mission, coupled with a strong belief in yourself and in a power greater than yourself, the possibilities of reinventing your life and transforming who you are now into who you can become are unlimited.

This book is designed to empower you with the secret process of success used by those who not only talk the talk, but more importantly, walk the walk.

You will go through step-by-step proven methods to transform your life and experience the health, wealth, and happiness we all want. I found every chapter inspiring and enlightening, as I'm sure you will.

These people have accomplished many tremendous things in their lives, and they are sharing the things that they have learned along the way with you. Read it with an open mind and an open heart.

The first volume of Multiple Streams of Inspiration changed lives and this book will change your life; I guarantee it.

— Les Brown

Multiple Streams of Inspiration

Volume 2

MULTIPLE STREAMS OF INSPIRATION
Enlightening, Empowering, Encouraging, Inspiring

© 2009 Wimbrey Training Systems

Manufactured in the United States of America

For information, please contact:

Wimbrey Training Systems
8708 Woodfell Court
Dallas, TX 75249

www.JohnnyWimbrey.com

info@JohnnyWimbrey.com

ISBN 978-1-60743-197-8

1 2 3 4 5 6 7 8 9 10

Contents

Winners Make It Happen!

Johnny Wimbrey

People of mediocre ability sometimes achieve outstanding success because they don't know when to quit. Most men succeed because they are determined to.
— George E. Allen

I have heard that one of the greatest regrets of people on their deathbeds is that they didn't take more risks in life. Isn't that mind blowing? To think of all the things that you could regret, one of the greatest is wishing that you had taken more risks. Not I wish I would have spent more time with my children or family or maybe even taken more elaborate vacations. I wish I had taken more risks.

It took me a while before I got the revelation. How could not taking risks be so devastating? I thought about this, and it finally came to me: To take the risk requires but a moment; not taking risks becomes a lifestyle. You have to do what others don't, to have tomorrow what others won't. Average people don't take risks, and average people live average lives.

> *He has not learned the lesson of life who does not every day surmount a fear.*
> — Ralph Waldo Emerson

Winners are not afraid to take risks because they understand that to win they must go further than the rest are willing to go. Risk takers are more afraid of being average than they are of being ridiculed by spectators. The only people who never fail are those who never try. You must do something different. You must be willing to go further than you've ever gone before. Dig deeper, push harder, and take more risks than you've ever taken before. And I promise you *will* go further than you've ever experienced before.

Wilma Rudolph was the twentieth of twenty-two children. Her premature birth started her off on shaky ground, even more than the poverty she was born into. The doctors doubted her survival. Then when she was four years old, she contracted double pneumonia, polio, and scarlet fever. Again doctors doubted she would ever walk without braces. Her paralyzed left leg hampered her gait, but not her spirit. At age nine, she removed the metal leg brace she had been dependent on and began to walk without it. By thirteen she had developed a rhythmic walk. Doctors said it was a miracle. That same year she decided to become a runner. At this point, no one doubted it, but they knew she would never win. She entered a race, and she came in last. For the next few years, every race she entered, she came in last. Everyone told her to quit, but she kept on running. One day she actually won a race. And then another. She began to win more than she lost. Then she won every race she entered. Eventually this little girl, a frail preemie, who was told she would never walk again, who was told she would never win a race, went on to win three Olympic gold medals.

A winner is not one who never fails, but one who *never quits!*

The Me Factor

In my training seminars I speak about the "You Factor." What is the difference between your colleague consistently making "Top Salesman of the Month" and you? Why does your brother excel in athletics while you sit on the bench? Why are you on the outside looking in? The "You Factor." You have the abilities and just as much talent, but you haven't decided to work at it, or go for it, or train hard, or build your confidence, so *you* hold the reins. In this section, I want to twist those words and the ideas 360 degrees. We'll end up in the same place, but the phrasing will be different.

I have been very fortunate to meet tens of thousands of outstanding and incredible individuals from around the world through seminars and trainings that I've conducted. It amazes me to see and meet individuals who have overcome the most devastating adversities. Some smile and are full of energy. You would never know the obstacles and trials they've endured. Somehow these individuals were able to overcome life's hardships and understand how paramount it is to be victorious over any and all situations. I was told this story of one woman (I'll call her Nancy) who was virtually abandoned by her mother at age nine. She became the mother to her six-year-old and three-year-old brothers. She had to avoid the landlord, steal food, and protect, comfort, and entertain her brothers. Her alcoholic mother would show up at the apartment every so often with a different man in tow. After screaming at her daughter to clean up the mess, she'd disappear into a back room. Some of the male visitors gave them money. Some simply looked at them with a blank stare. Eventually, they went to live with their maternal great-grandmother. When she died, the children were sent to different orphans' homes.

But Nancy was determined not to end up like her mother. She hung out in libraries, reading as many books as she could. When she could attend school, she devoured the lessons and emulated her teachers. Nancy knew she was as good as anyone else. She just didn't have quite as many pretty things. She pretended she would become a gifted singer, who would be on TV, admired by everyone. She dreamed she would become a famous surgeon, saving the lives of poor children. She visualized she would become a great teacher, helping the disadvantaged (just like herself). And guess what? She became a great teacher and a gifted singer. Not on TV, but making a difference in the lives of the disadvantaged and poor.

> *The art of being wise is the art of knowing what to overlook.*
> —William James, *The Principles of Psychology*

Anyone who sees such victory is amazed and wonders how one could endure so much and yet be completely healed spiritually, physically, and emotionally. How can someone who has been through so much devastation and terrible experiences be on top of the world? Then you have those who have experienced similar tragedies but are obviously stuck in the bondage of anger, denial, or depression. That young woman's brothers did not survive the hardships of their circumstances. One committed suicide; the other lives in an alcoholic stupor, a homeless bum.

So how do the ones who survive do it? The answer is simple, ladies and gentlemen. Attitude is a choice. The only difference, from those who triumphed over adversity and those who are wandering in the pits of depression is the individual's fight to resurrect.

I call this the "Me Factor."

Here's my personal example of the Me Factor. I am the youngest of three boys. My oldest brother Lawrence (Larry) is two years older than I am; then there's Willie, who is eleven months older than I am. We were all brought up under the exact same circumstances. We all had the same father, and we all had the same mother. We all ate the same food, and we all had the same economic status. The only difference between us was the Me Factor. Each of us chose different avenues to how we responded to our situation.

My brother Larry is currently in prison for the third time serving a forty-year sentence for aggravated robbery. My brother Willie has been in the ministry since he was eighteen years old and will become the principal of a public junior high school at the age of thirty. I speak to tens of thousands of people each year, encouraging and empowering the masses to experience true mental, spiritual, and physical wealth. How did three brothers who were raised in the exact same environment turn out with totally different futures? The Me Factor.

I love both my brothers with all my heart. We experienced many events from which most would not have made it out alive. Willie made his choices, early in life, by refusing to become a product of his environment. Somehow Willie decided to stand for what was right. He was able to say no to the many temptations we suffered and didn't make the mistakes that Larry and I did. Although we all had the exact same opportunities to make the exact same decisions, our choices to act on them were our own options. None of us is better than the other; we're all just different. Although I never robbed anyone at gunpoint, there are things that I participated in that deserve prison time; but I decided to change before I got caught.

We three brothers are a lot alike. All three of us are very compassionate individuals who would give the shirts off our backs to help someone else, and our parents are the exact same way. There are things that we say and do that are just alike, but although we had the same opportunities to decide right from wrong, the choices that we made were our own individual ones. The way a person responds to the cards dealt is a personal choice, and that is what I call the Me Factor.

I have trained sales organizations under the exact same principles. When I was an upper-level manager in the insurance industry, we always started out our week with a Monday morning sales meeting, discussing the previous week's production. I found that my top producers always had a great attitude and happy stories of how they had such an incredible week. On the extreme opposite side, I found that the agents who didn't have such a great week always had excuses—problems that were anything but their fault. Agents who had poor production complained about the leads, or the price, or how our products were inferior to the competition's. The fact of the matter is, every single agent in our division sold the exact same products; they all sold them at the exact same prices, while working from the exact same source of leads. The only difference between the top producers and the poor producers was the individual. Instead of wondering what they were doing wrong, they were focused on how the company and everything else was wrong. They should have been asking the top producers for wisdom and advice. They all were in the exact same office, under the exact same management, being trained by the exact same leaders. Why did they not all have the exact same result?

People who are on the bottom tend to point the finger at everyone else; it's never their fault. A wise person is one who applies taught knowledge, and a fool is one who has the knowledge but refuses to apply it. Although many can be exposed to the exact same teachings and principles, the end result will ultimately be determined by the individual's choice of actions. This is the Me Factor.

Instigators, Spectators, and Participators

There are three types of people in the world:

1. Instigators—those who talk about things happening.
2. Spectators—those who watch things happen.
3. Participators—those who *make* things happen.

Those who like to talk about things happening focus on problems. They are instigators and have no problem stirring up messes. They're always willing to throw gasoline onto any fire. Quick to talk about the problems, they are hardly ever compelled to search for solutions. They are the ones likely to be talking about how things could have been better. Individuals in this particular category don't possess the right answers, but they feel that they are qualified to point out the wrong answers.

Instigators are very unlikely to be on the inside of any major decision-making process. They are always the ones on the outside, wondering and complaining about what's going on inside. They have no desire to be in the game, but they always want to know what's going on. They love to participate in tailgate parties. They are not interested in actually seeing what's going on, but they're always close enough to at least hear the noise. They will smile in your face to get a free ride. Instigators are people pleasers. They always try to please others at any cost.

Then you have your spectators. These are the ones who watch things happen. Individuals in this particular group will get as close as they can to the game but will never join. They are just there to watch. Instigators and spectators have some similarities. They both are talkers with no desire to get in the game. Because an instigator is usually only on the outside, wondering what's going on inside, his or her information is usually passed on by a spectator.

Spectators actually see and witness the game firsthand; they have to see what's going on with their own eyes. Spectators can be very opinionated and sometimes even abusive. Spectators come to see two things. They want to see someone win, and they want to see someone lose. Although they claim to be loyal, spectators are known to turn on their own team in a split second. They are very emotional and quick to react. Even though in most cases they are not qualified to participate in the game, they are quick to criticize and judge the participants. Spectators need supervision and direction.

Finally you have your participators, the 5 percent who actually make things happen. These are the ones who are willing to get in the game. They are the ones in or on the field participating. Unlike the instigators and spectators, 90 percent of a participant's effort is dedicated to preparation for the game. They work hard practicing and perfecting their skills. They're constantly focused on winning. They are always prepared and willing to face any challenge.

Participants talk about solutions, not problems. They make things happen by addressing challenges with solutions. They are trained to ignore instigators and spectators. Regardless of what's going on around them and regardless of all the hype, they never get out of position. Participants are team players. They understand that breaking focus could bring harm to their fellow participants. There is no time for foolishness; they are focused on making things happen.

Each individual has the personal task of figuring out which category he or she falls in. You must make your decision today! Are you an instigator, always finding yourself talking about things that are happening? Are you a spectator, constantly watching things happen from a distance? Are you a participant in the game, focused on the end result (which is to win) and constantly bettering yourself by sharpening your skills and preparing to make things happen?

Win!

Anyone who looks hard enough for an excuse will find one. Do not let your past determine your future, because where you've been has nothing to do with where you're going. Speak life into your future and not death because whatever you say, you'll have. You must determine and be willing to accept that every individual has friends and foes. It is your personal responsibility to distinguish between the two and to disconnect from all that is holding you back. You possess the God-given mental ability to choose your destiny by every action that you display. Choose to be a winner today by seeing yourself at the top tomorrow. Think like a winner, believe that you are a winner, tell yourself that you are a winner, and you will win! Every day that you wake up is another day to *make it happen*!

I would rather lose in a cause that will some day win, than win
in a cause that will some day lose!
—Woodrow T. Wilson

It is never too late to walk into a new future. I used to think that it was too late for me to change my life because of all the baggage from my past. Then I learned why they call it the past . . . because it's behind you. It takes only one second to make a decision, and it takes only one step to start a journey of a thousand miles. Today is your first day; now take your first step. Make it happen! Welcome to your future!

If I can do it, anyone can.

About the Author

A young, dynamic, motivational success coach, known nationally for his record-breaking achievements, Johnny Wimbrey has trained and encouraged hundreds of thousands of people via radio, television, seminars, and events across the globe. Johnny's inspirational story of overcoming life's adversities has empowered the masses for greatness. He speaks on issues such as overcoming adversity, youth enrichment, mental breakthroughs, and entrepreneurship, to name just a few.

Johnny's young life was marked by one of his first memories of living in a shelter for battered women. Then he grew up as a young drug dealer on the hardcore streets. After several near-death experiences, he decided it was time to "flip the switch," and he refused to let his past determine his future. At the age of twenty, and with no experience, he became a temporary licensed insurance agent. In fewer than two years, Johnny found himself training experienced regional managers to recruit, manage, and teach sales development skills for well-known national agencies. After recognizing the high demand for his services, Johnny decided to use his skills for a higher purpose. His passion is to create success stories by helping others experience financial, spiritual, and emotional wealth.

Johnny has been featured and shared the stage with world-famous Les Brown, Zig Ziglar, Brian Tracy, Jim Rohn, Dr. John Gray, Dr. Denis Waitley, William E. Bailey, and Tavis Smiley, as well as many other great speakers, authors, and noted authorities from around the world. Founder and president of Wimbrey Training Systems, Johnny's message will challenge you to find your Inner Winner.

Inspiration

Ellie Drake

To understand the Principle of Liberty, first become aware of its context. This principle encourages us never to take for granted external liberty, ithin which we can create a life of success and fulfillment. To have such a life, we must also have internal freedom to such an extent that we can unleash our willingness to create success.

Perhaps you will find this story liberating and inspiring. If the story succeeds, then the Principle of Liberty will always hold great meaning for you.

It was 5 a.m. I washed my face with lukewarm water and looked at myself in the mirror, catching the light behind my dark, almond-shaped eyes. I placed the mandatory scarf on my head, attempting to cover what seemed at the time to be too much hair. I picked up a bag filled with books and started walking with my mom along a steep dirt road about two miles from our first destination. Out of our house, to the right, then about one hundred yards, and then a sharp turn to the left. My favorite part of this first small road was a little creek, perhaps two feet wide. The sound of water going down the creek helped prepare me for the road ahead. One step at a time. Sometimes I would come back to reality when the sweet yet tired voice of my mom would say, "Faster, Elham." (Elham is my Persian name. It means inspiration.) I would speed up to walk alongside my mom, all the while inhaling the cold crisp morning air of the small town called Karadje, which lies fifty miles from Tehran, the capital of Iran, the country where I was born. We would walk the two miles every day to the top of what seemed to be a neverending dirt road. Then I would catch a bus and ride into Tehran, where my parents had decided I would attend middle school. I guess you could say that we were middle class. I knew that my parents worked hard, and they accepted nothing but excellence from me and my future.

To keep my mind entertained during the very cold winter mornings, or the hot, dry days of summer, I would focus on one goal. As I walked up that familiar dirt road, I would teach myself one English word. It didn't matter which word, as long as it sounded like a person from Texas, Florida, New York, or California could understand it. Those were the only states I knew the names of at that time. I had much more to learn, in many subjects, so I stuck to my practice—one word per day, across two miles. "Sky. That's S K Y. Got it!" As long as I repeated the spelling forty to fifty times, I would be able to remember my new word. I hoped that I was pronouncing it correctly. The next day, "Light. That's L I G H T." The day after, "Food. F O O D." Then, "School. S C H O O L." One day I almost gave up. It took an extra day and two additional miles to get this one down: "T A B L E!" Why isn't it spelled T A B E L? I wondered.

Word after word, thought after thought, dream after dream, hope after hope! I must say I believed in the principle of "You must first believe it before you see it." I believed that one day I would be able to walk on a road paved not with dirt, but with gold.

By the time I was fourteen, we had moved to Tehran and lived in a small basement apartment. One day when I got home from school, I found my mom and dad sitting at the small kitchen table. They asked me to sit with them, and my dad explained that they had decided to immigrate to America. Those words were so sweet to my ears that I still remember how they sounded. After all, America was the synonym for Paradise. It was a place I would dream about before I went to sleep. It was the land of liberty and opportunity.

With the help of a very good friend, my father traveled to Cyprus to apply for a United States visa. His first attempt failed, but he had made his decision. When he tried again a few months later, his application was accepted. He left Iran shortly after that and went to Florida. He then hired an attorney and started the process of bringing my mom, brother, and me to America. The process with immigration went very slowly. At least a year and a half had passed. He missed us, and we missed him, but we had no choice other than to wait. One morning when my brother and I woke up, my mom told us that we were going to Dubai to see if we could get a visa. When she told my dad of her plan over the phone, he strongly opposed it. He said that it would be impossible for the three of us to get visas. However, my mom had run out of patience. She wanted to go to Dubai, and that was the end of the story. Two days later we left Tehran, arriving in Dubai at night. Before the sun came up, we were headed for the American embassy. Once there, at 4 a.m., we discovered that hundreds of people were already ahead of us. When the embassy opened at 7 a.m., they started taking people to one of only four American consul officials present. In front of each consul's booth stood a translator to relay the official's questions into Farsi for the applicants, and then give their answers to the consul in English.

Over the course of many hours, we saw that the only people being granted visas were the very few elderly. Hundreds of other applicants had walked out of their interviews with a deep sadness on their faces, still holding their passports, which meant that their applications had not been accepted.

Finally, in the middle of the afternoon, our number was called. As we started walking toward the consul, I was suddenly greatly inspired. I told my mom that we did not need a translator; I had decided to speak to the consul myself. I could see the worry in my mother's eyes, yet she accepted my proposal. We walked through the booth and toward the tall, blond American consul who held the key to our future. I still get butterflies when I think about that life-changing moment. He was studying our handwritten application, which I had filled out with the help of a dictionary. I spoke to him in broken English, "You must be tired; you have been working from the morning until now." He looked at us with an expression of acknowledgment and granted us a small, yet comforting, smile. He then asked me a few questions. My response to most of them was "Repeat, please?" When he asked why we wanted to come to America, I replied that we wanted to come to America because it was free. Actually, what I meant to say was that we wanted to come to America because it was the "Land of the Free."

After just two or three minutes, he looked at us and said, "You can go now. I will keep your passports. Come back at five o'clock, and you will have your visas."

It took us a few seconds to realize that we were awake and not dreaming. What a strange feeling. A dream for a better future, for a better life, a dream and a chance to change your family's future for generations to come. We walked out of the booth and a huge group of people ran after us, asking what our secret was. I have thought about that moment often, and I still don't know the answer to their question. Maybe the consul was just in a good mood, or maybe he felt the depth of the desire that was burning within us. I only know that I am forever grateful to those people, who are the reason I was able start my life in this country. I know that I am forever grateful to my dad for his sacrifice, to my mom for her courage, and to the American consul for his willingness to share his beautiful America with a girl from Tehran. Two months later we touched down at Miami International Airport, and I was reunited with my father. It had been nearly two years. At the moment we stepped out of the terminal building, I made a promise to myself that one day I would be a great asset to this country. My wish to fulfill that promise remains as strong as ever.

We drove north in a car that seemed splendid to me, though now when I think back, I realize it was probably the least expensive car in the state of Florida. In my teenage mind, I had hoped my father would greet us with a bag full of American chocolate cookies, or perhaps Big Macs, which my high school friends and I had always dreamed about. Instead, my father pulled over to the side of the highway and turned toward the back seat to present me with something totally unexpected. He stared into my eyes and said, "I want you to look back at the bridge that you have just crossed. I want you to burn that bridge. Because in spite of all the challenges that you may go through, you have just entered a country where if you have a dream and are willing to take consistent, persistent actions toward your dreams, you will achieve them in this land of opportunity." He paused to let those words sink in. Then he added, "If you are willing to fly like an eagle, America will be the wind beneath your wings."

Years later, when I left the United States for the first time and returned a few days later, as I walked through Customs I noticed the big banner ahead of me that said, "Welcome to the United States." At that moment my heart truly skipped a beat. I felt so blessed to be an American citizen and to live in a country where I have the *liberty* to pursue my passions, as well as the chance to actually achieve them. For that, I am forever grateful. And I have always remembered both the context and the content of this principle. There must be a place of freedom and one must hold onto the willingness to fly.

About the Author

Bursting onto the scene as an inspirational speaker from a series of seven-figure successes with several businesses, Ellie Drake is in demand because her message is motivational to many different groups. She both inspires entrepreneurs and empowers women; her message is inspirational to Fortune 500 executives as well as to budding business owners taking their first steps on a path toward achieving prosperity.

Her deep understanding of the keys to success combined with her heartfelt compassion elicits a genuine reaction in everyone who attends her motivational seminars. Among her other businesses, she currently leads the largest online paid-membership community for entrepreneurial women. This savvy businesswoman, in-demand inspirational speaker, doctor, and inspiration to men and women around the globe is a multidimensional success. She maintains a demanding schedule of personal appearances as well as a series of websites designed to assist individuals, each offering insights, newsletters, and products designed to help people achieve their personal best. As an immigrant to the United States, Ellie Drake has found inspiration in the American dream. Over the past fifteen years, she has become living proof of the power still left in that dream. For booking information, please visit www.elliedrake.com.

Excelerate

Vernice Armour

It was hot inside the cockpit. We were flying three hundred feet above the desert floor in the middle of a combat zone, and the sweat was rolling down my face. Reaching under my visor, I tried to use the back of my glove to wipe off the neverending stream. It was starting to roll into my right eye, and I swiped as quickly as I could, but I didn't have time to focus on it. I didn't even want to blink because I needed to stay focused on the land below. We were in hostile territory and quickly approaching a city. I sensed danger everywhere.

My attack helicopter section was escorting a convoy of about fifteen military vehicles as they drove cautiously down the road. They suddenly came to a stop when they should have kept a steady pace pushing forward. The clouds of sand and dust hung in the air as the convoy commander called us on the radio, telling us that a Marine in the lead vehicle had spotted something suspicious on the side of the road. It was a suspected improvised explosive device.

Our helos pushed forward and out. I looked into the camera sights to see as far up the road and terrain as I could. One helo would stay close to the convoy as the other flew farther ahead to scan over the horizon. We had to keep our eyes on the scene and on what lay ahead. Marines jumped out of the vehicles to provide security around the perimeter of the convoy. Even though the suspicious object was up ahead, everyone still had to keep up their awareness of the immediate surroundings, preparing for an attack from any angle.

In our daily lives, we all experience obstacles in our paths, seemingly blocking us from moving forward. Imagine that you are headed to the local mall. You turn into the parking lot, and before you can drive fifty feet, you encounter an obstacle in your path—a speed bump. What do you do as you approach the speed bump? What you always do. Slow down the car, and as the front wheels hit, let the car roll the rest of the way over the bump, then press on the accelerator to keep moving forward.

A funny thing happens as you clear the speed bump. You scan ahead for your parking spot. You aren't even focused on the obstacle! Instead, you stay focused on your next goal. You have just run smack dab into my core belief: *Acknowledge the obstacle, but* don't *give it power!*

The analogy of the speed bump isn't meant to diminish the almost larger-than-life obstacles we sometimes face. The point I want to impress upon you is the *process* used to overcome the obstacle. The process of overcoming that speed bump is the same process that can be used to overcome any obstacle we face in our personal and professional lives.

What was the actual process? You already had a something in mind. A desire, a dream, a goal. Step one: You acknowledge the obstacle that appears in your path of accomplishment. When the Marines saw something suspicious in the road, they stopped, but they still scanned forward through our eyes, the eyes in the sky. Acknowledgment is a key step. The type of obstacle determines the next step you take. The Marines had to come to a complete stop while we kept flying out and forward to see what was up ahead.

Step two: You stop, slow down, keep moving forward, or pick up the pace. In the first scenario, the Marines needed to stop. They used other resources to keep their momentum moving forward as well as staying "excelerated" mentally. In the second example, the car slowed down but kept moving forward as you scanned for the parking spot. You slowed down, but you were also mentally moving ahead. You cleared the obstacle and continued forward.

I learned many life lessons while in the middle of a war zone, faced with life and death decisions every day. I have adapted those lessons to my life back here in the States. One of the major takeaways was the importance of acknowledging the obstacles without giving them power. We always had to continue with the mission. Our lives and the lives of the men and women on the ground depended on it. Your life and your success or lack thereof depends on your ability to clear obstacles that present themselves in your life.

I enlisted in the Army reserves at the age of nineteen while going to college. My childhood dream was to be a cop who rode a horse downtown. That's right, I wanted to be in the mounted patrol. I still laugh every time I say it. I became a police officer at the age of twenty-two, right after my junior year. I finished my career as a police officer riding a Harley Davidson downtown, so I guess you could say I rode a steel horse.

Next on the list? Attack helicopter pilot! I became a Marine Corps officer and naval aviator, serving two tours in the Iraq war. I was recognized by the Department of Defense as America's first African American female combat pilot. During my last tour as a diversity liaison officer for Headquarters Marine Corps, another dream surfaced and started becoming a reality. Professional speaker!

Now, I travel around sharing my stories and experiences of leadership and teamwork on and off the battlefield. I talk about combat in corporate America, winning the war for our kids' futures, and winning the war for talent in today's top companies.

Did I have any obstacles? Of course. Who doesn't have obstacles? I can always count on a few people asking me that question. It's the one everyone always seems to want to know. It was tough making it through police academy. It was tough making it through officers' candidate school to become a Marine. It was tough making it through flight school to become a combat pilot. Yes, I had obstacles, but even the average white guy has obstacles.

People also love to ask me if I suffered from racism and sexism. I quickly reply that I don't know. I *don't* know why some people didn't like me. They might not have liked that I was black. Sure. They might not have liked me because I was a woman, sure. They might not have liked me because I was happy in the mornings. Or laughed all the time. Or could bench press more than they could. I didn't know, and honestly, I didn't care. Why some people didn't like me was their problem. All I wanted and needed to do was focus on the goal. To do that, I had to acknowledge the obstacle and not give it power. I gave my power to accomplishing my goals. As my granny would say, "Anything worth having is worth working for!"

So how did I end up shooting missiles and flying helicopters three hundred feet above the desert floor? I learned how to *excel*erate! I learned how to take my thoughts and actions to the next level. Nothing I have ever accomplished in life happened overnight, even though I used to wish it could, especially when it came to staying in shape or losing weight. But I realize through the help of those like Jim Rohn and Jeff Olson that it's the small decisions we make every day that make the huge difference. The things that are easy to do—and easy *not* to do.

Excelerated passion was my key. Imagine a huge dam holding back many thousands of pounds of water with a base of concrete thicker than a football field. Now imagine a small hole cut into the dam. What does the water shooting out right at the point of exit look like? When I researched the Hoover Dam, the second highest dam in America, I learned that during peak time, the water passing through its generator could fill up fifteen 20,000-gallon swimming pools in one second.

Now, imagine again what that water looks like shooting out. Then imagine what it looks like a mile downstream. Barely a trickle, right? We want to have the energy of the water right as it shoots out with the most force. The water goes from static to moving faster than we could imagine in an instant. It also slows down very quickly. In our lives, we want our energy to be focused on our goals in that moment of exceleration.

Passion—it's that stuff deep down inside you. You're good at it, everyone tells you you're good at it, and you *know* you're good at it. It's itching to get out of you. If you don't do it, you don't feel complete. You were born to do it.

That passion is yours and yours alone. It can also be looked at as your blessing. Blessings aren't for us to keep. They're for us to share. So what is your purpose *in* your passion? By that I mean, how are you supposed to share your blessing with me, everyone around you, everyone on this planet? What purpose did the universe have in giving you this passion or blessing? You've seen the books talking about purpose, such as the *Purpose Driven Life*. I'm sure you have heard people wonder aloud about their purpose in life. Well, I believe that our passions have a lot to do with our purposes.

Finally, what are the positive steps to bringing our passions to life? What are the many decisions we have to make every day? What is the attitude we need to possess? What is the thought process? What is the inner desire behind the success? What's your *why*? Why do you want it? Is your why big enough to make you work hard enough? To make you find ways over all the obstacles? To bring you to the other side in full exceleration?

What other lessons have I learned from all my experiences? I can't go into depth at this time, but I'd love to share more of my insights and lessons learned. You can always get more information on my website, www.VerniceArmour.com, and via my monthly newsletters. Here's a quick overview of a few of my lessons.

Excelerated Faith. You have to have faith in yourself. You have to have faith in something greater than yourself. Faith brings you through those lonely, tough, and trying times we all have at some point in our lives.

Excelerated Leadership. You have to be able to lead yourself before you can lead others. What character traits should you possess to be that excelerated leader?

Excelerated Diversity. If we want to excelerate in our industry, we must realize diversity is a strategic advantage.

Excelerated Teamwork. I didn't get here by myself, and I'm not going anywhere by myself. The team got me here, and the team will get me there.

Excelerated Legacy. We, our society, are realizing the fruits of a strong legacy. We must give back and continue to build on where we are.

You are here because of the decisions you have made in the last year, the last three years, the last five years, all the years you have been making decisions in your life, no matter how small you feel they have been. Today, you have the chance to excelerate your life to the next level no matter where you are. Your success is absolutely dependent on you and your commitment to keep pushing forward to your goals no matter what obstacle lies in your path.

The *o* in obstacle stands for opportunity. Obstacles are just opportunities with a little extra challenge attached to them. Think of obstacles as divine guidance put in our way to put us back on the right path. So many things have happened in my life that I didn't understand at the time. Those experiences are responsible for you reading these words right now.

For example, after combat operations slowed down during my first tour, the training started to pick back up. I found out we were going to have a tactics test. My heart sank because I hadn't been studying like I needed to. The day of the test came, and fifteen minutes into it, I knew I wasn't doing so hot. The next day, it was confirmed. I had bombed, and I was devastated.

I felt like I had let many people down. I'd let my family down, women down, the Marine Corps down. I'd let myself down. But most of all, I felt like I'd let those guys in the squadron down because I didn't show them the full potential of what I or any other woman or minority could do. I had let down the standard I needed to uphold. The next week, I took the test again and passed with flying colors, but the damage had been done. I wasn't even close to being put on the fast track. The rest of my tour, two and a half more years, was successful. At the end of that tour, I was moved to the East Coast, to Quantico, Virginia.

It had to have been about 10:00 p.m., and I was sitting in the officers' club parking lot talking to a bud of mine. She had been in the Marine Corps for more than twenty-six years, and I knew there wasn't anything I could tell her that she wouldn't understand. She had been the first black woman to become a chief warrant officer five in the history of the Marine Corps.

I told her all the things that were on my heart. I told her things I never would have shared with others, just because they didn't seem like a big deal when I said them out loud, but over years of dealing with them, they had become a heavy weight. I started talking about the tactics test and how deeply I regretted failing. I felt that had I passed and done well, I would have been put on the fast track. I felt I would have gone to WTI or top gun school, been a test pilot, and been back in Iraq with my team, my squadron, supporting the men and women on the ground. Then I stopped when I realized, yeah, I would have been back in Iraq right then. And then I wouldn't have met the people I had and experienced the things I'd experienced in the last year.

Slowly, a little window in my head was opening, and the sun rays were shining through. I wouldn't have gone to the Women of Color in Technology conference and made the decision to go for my true passion, speaking. I wouldn't have been sitting at a desk to answer the phone when my mom called on that memorable Wednesday afternoon.

She had sounded a little sad. I could always tell when she was feeling down. Dad was in the hospital. His blood count was low so he was having routine blood work done. It looked like he was going to be in the hospital on Saturday, her birthday. She asked if I was coming home, and I said no, that I couldn't get the time off. After we hung up the phone, I bought a ticket home.

I walked in the door on Saturday morning much to my mom's surprise. I wiped her tears and asked what was for dinner. A little while later, we headed up to see Dad. We got there around 2:00 p.m. He was surprised and happy to see me. "Hey, baby! How're you doing?! I didn't know you were coming home this weekend!" It was great seeing him. He was a Marine and had served two tours in Vietnam. He was my favorite Marine.

By 6:07 p.m. he had passed away. It was a blessing to be at his side.

Les Brown has an amazing saying, and one I found particularly on point: "You can't see the picture when you're in the frame." Sitting in that car, I asked myself one question. Was it worth the sacrifice? Without hesitation, I answered "yes." Had I to do it all over again, I wouldn't change a thing, not even failing that tactics test. When you're going through rough times, and it seems like the whole world is bearing down on you, hold strong and stay committed and *excel*erate. Obstacles are opportunities, opportunities with a little extra challenge attached. Obstacles are divine guidance put in our way to put us back on the right path. Acknowledge the obstacles, but *don't* give them power.

About the Author

As featured on *Oprah Winfrey*, CNN, *Tavis Smiley*, NPR, and other shows and networks, Vernice Armour's dynamic style and presentation methods have affected many organizations and individuals. Vernice stands on many shoulders, a strong legacy, and is highly sought after for her message of *EXCEL*erated Leadership™ and *EXCEL*erated Success through her unique insight and life strategy: "From Zero to Breakthrough!™"

Vernice knows a little something about focus, commitment, and defying the odds. After accomplishing her dream of becoming a police officer, she decided, at age twenty-four, to become an officer in the Marine Corps and a combat pilot. Only three years later, she became America's first African American female combat pilot by the Department of Defense. Vernice completed two tours in Iraq.

Among her accomplishments, Vernice has been awarded for being a pioneering pilot and her role in technology and engineering. She was also the first African American woman on the Nashville Police Department's motorcycle squad, Camp Pendleton's 2001 Female Athlete of the Year, two-time titleholder in Camp Pendleton's annual Strongest Warrior Competition, and a running back for the San Diego Sunfire women's professional football team. Vernice's next book, *FlightPlan*, is due for release in early 2009.

Blueprint of a Dream

Bobby Minor

When I decided to write a chapter for this book, I was adamant about one thing. I would not tell you what you to do to bring your dreams to life. Rather, I would tell you what I did to bring my dreams to life.

In looking back at what I consider major dreams I've made into reality, I find they all pretty much fall into two categories. The first category consists of dreams I pursued "just because." They didn't really change my life or anyone else's. They were just things that I had always wanted to do. Let's call these personal dreams, or dreams of attainment. They include things like putting together my own semi-pro baseball team and winning the championship, learning to play ice hockey and being named league MVP, performing stand-up comedy and visiting New York. They meant something to me personally, were things I wanted to do, and I did them.

The rest of my dreams fall under the category of enhancement, meaning they enhanced my life or someone else's in various ways—financially, emotionally, spiritually, or in some other way that had a positive impact. For me, quitting my corporate sales job to launch my own magazine, creating new divisions within two Fortune 500 companies, and writing my first book, *Dream Big, Win Big!*, all fit in this enhancement category. Likewise, sharing the stage with legends like Les Brown and Zig Ziglar, coauthoring a book with Olympic gold medalist Lanny Bassham, and launching God Encounter Television also fit in this group.

Sometimes a dream can overlap both categories, personal and enhancement. For me, being able to fulfill a childhood dream of performing stand-up comedy actually fits both categories because it was something I had always wanted to do, and I actually got paid to do it.

As I began to dissect my dreams and chart them from beginning to end, a pattern emerged. There were commonalities in all of them, especially the enhancement dreams. Personal dreams are tricky in the sense that, in some of them, it may not be obvious what exactly took place in the process. Besides, it's also easier to put a personal dream on hold. For example, let's say you always wanted to visit Disney World as a child but never got to. Now that you have a family of your own, it's your dream to take them. But if you find that for some reason your plans fall through, chances are it won't be a big deal to say, "let's wait until summer." On the other hand, if it's your twelve-year-old daughter's dream to visit Disney World, and she has terminal cancer, you will do whatever it takes to make the trip. It's now an enhancement dream. Your motivation is much greater.

As I go through the different phases of bringing a dream to life, I want you to think from the perspective of an enhancement dream. If possible, I'd like you to think of a dream you brought to life, or perhaps one that you wanted to but didn't. See if you can identify how the following different components relate to your dream.

As I describe what I will call the Dream Machine, I am going to use the example of when I quit my corporate sales job with a shoe manufacturer to launch my own niche magazine. I left a base salary and benefits to walk out on my own with no financial backing. Sound crazy? Maybe it won't after we break it down. Almost every dream of mine, including this one, at some point started with an *inspiration*. This isn't the actual dream itself but the catalyst or spark that got my wheels turning. More times than not, it will be either some sort of pain or a cause, something that moves you.

For me, my inspiration came when I was sitting in a hotel room in Southern California during a thirteen-day sales trip. I realized at that moment how much I hated being away from my seven-year-old son for that long. I hated missing his baseball games because I had to travel and missing his golf tournaments because I had sales meetings. I wanted to be in control of my schedule and my time. I knew that as long as I worked for someone else, that would never be the case. My wheels were turning.

The next three components can occur independently of each other or simultaneously. In my case, they all happened almost instantaneously. The next part of the process is the *vision*. This is the dream itself. My dream was to launch my own business, set my own schedule, and never miss another one of my son's activities. This ties into the next component, my *motivation*, or *why*. Your why is what will get you going and keep you going. This may be the single biggest factor in determining whether you will see your dream through to completion. Your why has to be bigger than you, and big enough that you will not let anyone or anything come between you and your dream. Think of it this way: If your why don't make you cry, it's not big enough.

After that came the *calculation* phase. I started to formulate a plan and began doing research. I wanted to not only start my own business, but try to attach it to something I loved doing and to something I could do well. I knew that a perfect fit for me would be to bring golf and sales together. I loved golf and was good at sales.

After much consideration, I decided to launch a monthly junior golf magazine that would be 100 percent supported by advertising revenue. I spent several weeks doing my homework and coming up with a game plan. As things began to fall into place, I knew that this would provide the income I needed, so long as it was properly executed. I then reached the point of *realization*, the next step in the process, when I told myself, "I can do this!" This is where we cross over from testing the waters to actually starting to believe that our dream is achievable. This is also where the importance of our self-image kicks in. Keep this point fresh in your mind—your performance will never exceed your self-image.

Once I made it that far, I was rocking and rolling. But in truth, most dreams die either directly before or after the next step. The next step in bringing your dreams to life is actually quite simple, but many people never reach this point. You must make a *decision*. That's all it is. Decide. You have to transition from *I can do this* to *I'm going to do this*.

At some point, you have to decide that you are going to pursue your dream. But don't stop there. Follow me for a second. Three boys are sitting on a bridge overlooking a creek. Two of them decide to jump in. How many are left? If you answered one, you're wrong. The correct answer is three. You see, they only decided to jump. If half the people who let their dreams die do so because they never decide to pursue their dream, then the other half let their dreams die because they fail to take the next step, which in reality is the most important. These people decide to act, but they never take *action*.

You can sit around all day and talk about what you are going to do and even tell everyone how you've decided to finally chase down that dream, but brother, if you never take action, it will never happen. You can quote me on that.

This one key to success is what prompted me to come up with my signature quote: "It's not how many dreams you have; it's how many you bring to life." My dream truly began to take shape when I handed in my letter of resignation and walked out the door. There was no turning back. I took the first step. I took action.

I always like to remind myself that talk is cheap. And the old saying is true: A journey of a thousand miles begins with a single step. Once I quit my sales job and walked out the door, my journey had begun.

The next step is *implementation*, the period in which you begin to work your plan. For me, this is where it really got fun. I created a media kit, made some copies, and went out cold calling, trying to sell advertising in a magazine that did not yet exist anywhere other than in my dream. To all the entrepreneurs out there, and I'm speaking from experience, there's not a person alive who can or will sell your dream better than you. If I had hired a sales team to go out and sell my dream, I probably wouldn't be writing this today.

You don't have to be a salesman per se. Just share your dream with passion, and people will buy into it if it makes sense. The first ad I sold was my back cover. I sold it to a national golf shaft manufacturer that told me up front that it didn't do any "local" advertising. I'm glad I decided not to listen. After making that sale, I knew there was no stopping me! I was building momentum.

This led me to *continuation*, where I simply continued to implement my plan. This is also a point where you may need to evaluate and adapt if necessary. I continued to tell my story and sell advertising until I had enough money to begin printing. From the time I created my media kit to the day I had sold enough advertising to begin printing, just twenty-nine days had elapsed. In a little less than a month, I was ready to print the first issue of my magazine. I'll never forget the day I went to the printer to pick up the first run of magazines. A copy of my first issue, featuring my oldest son, Caleb, and PGA Tour player Sergio Garcia on the cover, hangs on my wall in a glass case. It is a daily reminder of my why and what can happen when I pursue my dreams.

That is when I reached *completion*. I had brought that dream to life. It was absolutely incredible to look back and think about that night in my hotel room in Southern California, where an idea was born, and then follow the road that led me to where I was, standing there holding a copy of my magazine. Not someone else's magazine. My magazine.

At this juncture, I reached the point of *evaluation*. I had to look back on the whole process and pat myself on the back for all the things I did right and honestly assess areas that needed improvement. I will never dwell on an area that comes up short, but I have to acknowledge it and recognize what I can do differently next time. Even though I list evaluation as the last step, after completion, in reality it needs to be done after each phase. I constantly evaluate and adapt when necessary. Keep in mind that it's impossible to connect the dots looking forward, but you can always connect them looking back.

When I began my quest to do my own thing, I would have never thought that the journey would lead me to some of the opportunities it has. That one magazine led to three regional editions, two in Texas and one in Florida; another magazine associated with the top regional junior golf tour in the United States; a national junior golf radio show that I cohosted with Valeria Ochoa from the Big Break; and a junior golf television show. I've interviewed more professional golfers and celebrities than I can list, people like Kathy Whitworth, Tom Lehman, Ivan Lendl, and George Lopez, just to name a few.

My point in saying all this is not to brag. It's merely to help you understand that even though our dreams may seem big initially, they have the potential to be much bigger than we can ever imagine. If you've ever been to a redwood forest, perhaps you'll understand. The redwoods soar to the heavens, and from the forest floor, you can't even see the treetops. But if you look on the ground, you just may find tiny cones containing even tinier seeds. The mighty redwoods all around you sprang from seeds just like that. This is the way of dreams. They hold more potential than we can fathom. But our dreams will remain just untapped potential unless we take that first step and act. That's what I did, and you can, too.

About the Author

Bobby Minor is a dynamic, passionate, anointed speaker, author, and navigator of life. He is a called voice for this generation as he travels across the country speaking at churches, corporations, colleges, concerts, and conferences. Bobby's theme, "Life Can Change," is evident no matter where he speaks because he is living, breathing proof that nothing and no one is beyond hope. Bobby is the author of *Dream Big, Win Big! The Lingering Look and Seven Other Ways Godly Men Cross the Line, Bringing Your Dreams to Life!* with Vernice Armour, and *With Winning in Mind for Salespeople,* with Lanny Bassham. He received his BA in Biblical Studies from Andersonville Seminary and is married, a father of three, and an associate pastor at Waves of Faith in South Fort Worth, Texas.

Creating the Fire Within

Matt Morris

After interviewing hundreds of wildly successful entrepreneurs, I've found one common thread that runs through them: The ability to harness a white heat of passion that spills out and gets all over the people around them. I'm sure you've been around people like that, people who just have a charisma that makes you feel good to be around them and leaves you feeling better about yourself after being in their presence.

That special charisma is what I call their *passion*. It's an intense emotion that drives them to succeed, a gut feeling that burns within them and fuels their inner being, their essence, to great achievement. It took me a while, but I learned the value of passion myself. Before I did, however, I had to experience extreme lows.

I can well remember the turning point in my life, the point at which I finally got it, when I finally made the mental shift and vowed that I would no longer accept mediocrity in my life. At that point I made the real commitment to creating the life of my dreams and living a life filled with passion. We're all motivated by either the avoidance of pain or the desire for pleasure. Unfortunately, what it took for me to have the lights turn on was an extreme amount of pain in my life. When I hit rock bottom, I finally woke up.

I started a business at twenty-one years old. Because of my lack of discipline and extreme lack of vision for my life, I was out of business within nine months. I found myself buried in approximately twenty thousand dollars in credit card debt. I was so broke, I couldn't afford to make the minimum payments on my credit cards or even pay rent.

After my failed entrepreneurial venture, I took a job as a pool salesman traveling in southern Louisiana in the sweltering heat of July and August. Because I didn't get paid commissions until the pool actually got installed, I ended up living out of my little red Honda Civic five to six nights a week, parking underneath shade trees so I wouldn't wake up being cooked by the sun.

Because I couldn't afford the luxury of staying in a motel with a shower, I bathed in gas station bathrooms. Late one night when I found myself in a city without an open gas station, I actually showered in the rain, standing underneath the runoff from the roof of a church.

I remember it as though it were yesterday. I got back in my car that night, laughing out loud at being the absolute definition of pathetic. I realized that I *had* to find a way to turn my life around.

That very night I popped in a cassette tape by a man who would soon become my mentor—Tony Robbins. Tony told his story of living out of a four-hundred-square-foot apartment, which, given my circumstances, actually sounded pretty luxurious to me. He told of going from living an average existence to earning more than a million dollars a year in personal income. One of the things he had done at an early age was to read more than seven hundred books in the field of personal development. He also talked about modeling other people and noted that to be a success, you simply needed to figure out what that successful person did and do the same thing.

I put two and two together and decided that I would, like Tony, start reading everything I could get my hands on that would help me train and develop myself into a success. I started spending every spare moment in bookstores, pouring myself into books on sales, wealth generation, leadership, motivation, communication skills, and anything else that would propel me forward.

I read at least one book every two or three days and was particularly influenced by one of Tony's books. He stressed the importance of writing lists of everything you wanted in life and assigning deadlines for achieving those things. The simple exercise of putting dreams and goals on paper opened up a whole new world of passion. I literally saw and believed that I could live the life of my dreams. I quickly learned that dreams are the fuel that fires your passion.

I began visualizing myself having and living the life of my dreams. I saw a world in which everything I wanted was possible for me. I visualized earning millions of dollars, being able to take exotic vacations around the world, contributing millions of dollars to charity, helping other people become financially free, and being a leader that other leaders would follow. Now, just eight years later, I have come to the complete understanding that the more you visualize your dreams, the more you harness your passion. I've also come to see that the more passion you live in your life, the more results you create.

I heard a saying many years ago that inspires me to this day and I suggest that you adopt it in your life as well if you desire to be a leader: "Get on fire for your passion and others will come from all over to watch you burn!"

It's that "getting on fire" that's allowed me to go from adversity to prosperity. It's my passion that's allowed me to be the top money earner in sales organizations with thousands of other salespeople, that's allowed me to travel all over the world, that's allowed me to help countless other people earn six-figure incomes, that's allowed me to generate millions of dollars and to be the CEO and founder of one of the largest personal development companies in the world, Success University.

Because of my passion for helping others achieve success, and our team's passion for making a difference in the world, we've been able to attract some of the greatest speakers, trainers, and authors in the entire personal development industry. We now generate millions of dollars in sales every year, but more important, we are helping people all over the world achieve financial and personal success in their lives. I now wake up every morning 100 percent committed to living every day of my life enjoying and giving to others God's gift of love, happiness, and passion. Not bad for a guy who lived out of his car and had to bathe in gas station restrooms.

Figure out what it is that can stir your blood. Discover what it is inside you that can create that white heat of passion in your life. Write down everything that you can imagine being possible for your life. Put down *everything* you could possibly want. To the side, give yourself a deadline for each item.

Some of your dreams may be extremely ambitious. You may not even believe you can achieve them now. But the simple act of putting them on paper will open up the possibilities for you to make them a reality. I can remember when I created my dream list and had no clue whatsoever how I was going to achieve those dreams. Now, just a few years later, I'm astonished by how many of those dreams have actually been realized.

Dream *big* dreams, and use those dreams to fuel your passion. Make a conscious decision to fuel your passion at every possible opportunity, and believe wholeheartedly that your dreams *can* become a reality. Success is sure to follow.

About the Author

As a former sergeant in the Marine Corps, Matt Morris leads the charge as president and CEO of Success University and its dedicated team. Originally from Arlington, Texas, he went to school at the University of Texas at Austin before successfully achieving his full-time career in network marketing. A twelve-year veteran of the network marketing industry, Matt has been responsible for building sales organizations totaling over 100,000 representatives worldwide. Previous to Success University, Matt not only became the top money earner in two network marketing companies, he built his own technology and marketing firm responsible for millions of dollars in revenues. His success story has been profiled on national and international radio and television.

His dedication and passion for training and developing others, commitment to remaining a student of personal development, and visionary leadership have led to the creation and success of Success University. For more information please visit www.successuniversity.com.

The Four Aces of Success

Jose De La Torre, Jr.

Name: Jose De La Torre, Jr.
Marital status: Married, with a six-month old baby
Age: 28
Birthplace: Elmhurst, Illinois
Education: GED (Get Every Dollar)

Before you read my advice on how to be successful, I would like to give you a snapshot of my life. The purpose is to show you that if I can do it, then anyone can. One thing I truly believe is that there is no such thing as luck. You create your own luck by working hard and doing the right things.

I was raised in a single-mother home. My mom did her best, but we lived around gangbangers. When I was seventeen, my life came to a screeching halt. I lived in a three-floor house with my mom and brothers on the top floor. My cousin and grandparents lived in the middle. A young couple with their baby lived in the basement level.

One of the rival gangs I fought with threw cocktail bombs into my grandparents' apartment. Fortunately, they were out of town at the time, and I was instantly put in protective custody. At the time, I was already in court fighting charges from months before. I was found guilty on charges of mob action and was sentenced to one year in an adult penitentiary. With good behavior, I was out in sixty-one days, the minimum time you can serve.

When I was released, I went on a job hunt and quickly found out that having a record was frowned upon. I caught a break at a local grocery store where my mom worked. I worked there for two years, gained experience, and applied at a local competitor. I was offered a position of grocery clerk. Well, the corporation wanted to let me go because of my criminal record, but I convinced the store manager to talk the company into giving me a chance. He did, and from that point on, I moved to dairy manager then to grocery manager within a year. I was the youngest manager in the whole corporation. At twenty I wasn't even able to go on the company's Vegas trip for managers.

I won't lie to you. It felt good to be finally given a chance. Later, I was given an even bigger opportunity to run a new store within the company. When I transferred to the new branch, once again my background came up. This time, my supervisor at the new store wasn't able to convince the corporation to keep me. I was back where I started.

Once again my life was at a halt. Every job I was offered paid seven to eight bucks an hour. I was getting more on unemployment! I looked in the local newspaper for a job. It was the first time I'd done that. There I saw a position advertised at fifteen dollars an hour, with no experience necessary, for office management.

I almost didn't call because I wasn't familiar with an office, but my girlfriend at the time—now my wife—pointed out that the company offered job training. I called to set up an interview and was hired on the spot. It was a fire-safety sales company. To make a long story short, in five years I moved to management, then to regional, then to VP of sales.

Today I own a couple companies, and I am currently putting one together as we speak. I'm not stuck up, but I believe I am an example to follow. I didn't let something like a criminal background or a lack of education hold me back. I believe I was put on this planet to inspire people to stop making excuses and instead to make it happen. I decided to be a Mexi-Can, not a Mexi-Can't. I wasn't going to be a product of my environment.

My passion is to be an author, to motivate others with my story. I also plan on being a big name in public speaking like Zig Ziglar and Johnny Wimbrey. I should warn you right now that some of the information I share in this chapter might offend you. But a leader tells you what you need to hear, not what you want to hear. I hope you take something from it, because I believe in what I write. I call my chapter "The Four Aces of Success." If you ask me which ace is the most important, I would have to say the ace of spades. But you'll need to keep reading to figure out why.

Ace of Hearts: Attitude

The ace of hearts represents attitude. I start with this one because unless you have a positive attitude, the rest of this chapter is worthless to you. Attitude is everything. A positive attitude will yield positive results, and a negative attitude will doom you to failure.

I do many speeches for people, and despite the recipe for success that I give to them, there is always a pessimist in the crowd. No matter how much I explain the "how to," this naysayer is already sold on failure and debates me. It gets to the point sometimes when I just want to say, "Hello, if you were the successful one, wouldn't you be doing the speech?" Sometimes I just have to tell the person,

"No matter how many times you debate me, I'm not going to say you're right."

I mean, if I did agree with these people, there'd be no point trying to teach. No matter what I say, pessimists have an excuse for why my method won't work, and they know it won't work because they already tried it. The key word there is "try."

In order to be willing to learn the "how to," you need to first change your pessimistic attitude. It takes a little trust to be willing to learn from another human being. But without that trust, we've got nothing. Think of a sports team. What is the point of disagreeing with the coach if he or she is the only one who can help you? If you've got a bad attitude, changing it into a positive attitude is the first thing you need to do if you truly want to be successful.

Here's the way I look at it: A poor attitude = poor health = poor habits = poor people *period!* That might sound harsh, but I firmly believe that people choose to be poor. I get a lot of criticism for my views, but I feel I can say it without offending people because I had no silver spoon in my mouth when I was born. I grew up in gangs, with just one parent and no father or father figure.

My siblings and I were raised on the free lunch program at school, and we received gifts from the shelter. We hated getting gifts from the shelter because it was always clothes. We were poor, but we still had high standards. And that was important, because ultimately we weren't going to be limited by negative thinking.

Let me explain. I believe the word "can't" is worthless. When we say we can't do something, we really mean we won't do something. My opinion is that "can't" should be removed from the dictionary. Think about it for a second. Is there anything a person can't do? I always get the pessimists with this one. He or she might say, well, I can't eat shellfish or I will die. That's an easy one. The person *can* still eat shellfish but has to consider the consequences. The point is not that the person can't eat shellfish but that the person won't eat shellfish because of the consequences.

Others will say something like, well, I can't swim. Why not get lessons? Or maybe someone will say, well, I can't find a job. But that's clearly wrong. There are always more jobs than workers. What people are really saying when they claim they can't get a job is that they just don't want the jobs with horrible pay and lousy benefits, or they don't want the job that requires them to work hard.

Everything you do is a choice. I've heard people say things like, "I really hate that guy. I would love to hit him, but I can't." Well, actually, yes, you can. But maybe you don't want to risk jail time. Or maybe you're afraid he'll light you up. But none of those things changes the fact that you can, in fact, punch the guy.

What about a woman who is in an abusive relationship? It always saddens and annoys me when battered women say something like, "I can't leave him, and besides, he'll change." Hey, the door is right there. Just walk, for God's sake. Because if one thing is certain, it is that a guy who is abusing you now is not going to change.

My point is that everything *can* be done. There really is no such thing as can't. All of this, of course, ties into your mindset and attitude. In the end, what you believe is true is true. If you believe you don't deserve success, you're right, because that's what you believe, and those beliefs will limit your performance. But that's looking at the issue in a negative light. Let's flip it around: High expectations equal high rewards. I knew from when I was a child that I would be successful some day. The difference between others and me is that my confidence followed me into my adult life.

Go to any playground and you'll usually see some kid crying because another kid called him names or made fun of him. Frantic parents will try to soothe the child with sorry clichés like, "Sticks and stones may break your bones, but words can never hurt you." Maybe it works and maybe it doesn't. But in the end, it's dead wrong. Words are powerful. They have meaning. And they can dictate the course of our lives.

I call the following group of words Glass Words. All of them have something in common—they're never used by successful, confident people.

Can't
Wish
Maybe
I don't know
Try
But
Hopefully
Think
Assume
Never
Would
Could

These are just a handful of words you should never use. Why not? Because your attitude is you. When you find yourself using this gibberish, you don't sound confident. In fact, it's pretty clear that you don't believe you will succeed. Instead of believing, you're wishing. I don't know of anyone who believes in genies, so why are we always wishing?

Look at Michael Jordan. Do you think for a minute that he said, "I hope I make it to the pros"? Of course not. Instead, he constantly told himself that he would make it to the pros and that he would win. Let's face it. You don't win six championships trying to win. You win six championships by going out and doing it.

Hoping? Why hope? It's a lot better just to make it happen.

To succeed you need to have a goal, a coach, and a plan. A man with no goals is not a man at all. Donald Trump doesn't go into a bank and say, "Hello, Mr. Banker, lend me money and hopefully my buildings will sell." He has a goal, he has a plan, and man, he has confidence.

Confidence is a huge part of the recipe for success. People want to follow confidence, and women want to be married to confident men. People buy from confident people. People go listen to motivational speakers who are confident, not to those who lack confidence.

Again, your attitude is you. Go out there and start telling people your plans; it shows confidence. Next time someone tells you good luck, reply that there is no such thing as luck and that you create your own success. Be positive all the time. Don't fake it. Enjoy life. And remember that sometimes life is tough, and sometimes obstacles get in our way. But also remember that it's not what happens to you that determines your success, but how you react to what happens to you.

I'd like to close this section with a quote by Marianne Williamson that I believe says it all:

> *Our deepest fear is not that we are inadequate. Our deepest fear is that we are powerful beyond measure. It is our light, not our darkness, that most frightens us. We ask ourselves, who am I to be brilliant, gorgeous, talented, and fabulous? Actually, who are you not to be? Your playing small doesn't serve the world. There's nothing enlightened about shrinking so that other people won't feel insecure around you. We are all meant to shine, as children do. We are born to make manifest the glory that is within us. It's not just in some of us, it's in everyone. And as we let our own light shine, we unconsciously give other people permission to do the same. As we are liberated from our own fear, our presence automatically liberates others.*

Ace of Clubs: Association

My next ace of success is the ace of clubs. The word "club" has many meanings, of course. It can mean a weapon, something you can use to knock someone on the head. Or a club can be a group of people with a common interest. That's the meaning I'm going to use here, because the ace of clubs is all about association.

What do I mean by association? Well, a mentor of mine, Dan Silva, once said to me, "Tell me who your friends are, and I will tell you who you are." That has stuck with me, and I can now confidently say that if you hang around losers, you are a loser. Sure, you can say, "Well, my friends are not me," but the truth is that who you associate with is who you become. When I was younger, I was given that advice by a probation officer. He used to say, "If it walks like a duck and looks like a duck, what is it?"

My associations at an early age were with gangbangers. Clearly, I wasn't paying attention to the very good advice I had been given. I had to learn the hard way. But I believe everything happens for a reason, and I believe I was supposed to be a gangbanger so that one day I could talk to young gangbangers and tell them to leave that lifestyle. I have credibility with them because I have been there firsthand.

Think about the associations in your life. If you were raised in a Nazi family, odds are you will become one, right? If you hang with gangbangers, Republicans, Catholics, Democrats, Christians, losers, successful people, you will start to share their beliefs. My point here is simple. Be careful who you associate with, because everyone in your life is either hurting you or helping you. This means the closest people in your life could be hurting you. It is up to you to stray away from "the masses or you will continue to be broke asses." Leaders change people's opinions but don't let others change theirs.

When you are on a path of success, the masses will try to keep you down. It's like the "crab in the bucket" analogy. What happens when a crab tries to escape from the bucket? The other crabs keep pulling it back in. Be careful who you listen to.

Let's imagine that you become successful in your endeavor. How is that going to make the others around you feel? In a sick way, they are hoping for your failure, because then they won't feel more insecure than they already do. I have had all kinds of "instigators" in my life, but the difference between me and others is that I chose not to listen. The simple lesson here is that if the person giving me advice is not where I need to be, why am I listening? Do you take legal advice from a mechanic? No. If you are having a heart attack, do you call your lawyer? No, of course you don't. Like Johnny Wimbrey says, "I associate myself with people who celebrate me, not tolerate me."

Ace of Diamonds: Achievement

My next ace of success is the ace of diamonds. Hey, if you're successful, the bling will come. Most of us want to be successful and to enjoy the comforts that come with it. But we must achieve in order to be successful. Wishing isn't going to make it so. I believe winning is everything. I once heard someone say that no matter what field you are in, always be in the top 10 percent. Being competitive gives you an edge over the masses.

Have you ever been passed over for a promotion, or maybe decided not to pursue a career-advancing job because you were afraid to compete with upper management? You know, that's a more common problem than you might think. Many people are scared to advance because they know the higher they go, the greater the chances they'll get in situations in which they'll have to fight for principles with people who don't like confrontation. They're scared that if they get those jobs, they'll have to say or do things that might get them fired.

I am an extreme alpha-male. That doesn't mean I want to crush people or fight with management. Let's face it. Most people don't like their boss. It may be some personal twitch the boss has, or it may just be that you think the boss is doing things that hinder the company's success. Well, my thought on this is that if you don't agree with the person who supervises you, than do something about it. Doing something about it doesn't mean getting people together and talking about this person, or trying to get him or her fired. When I talk about doing something about it, I mean work harder and get noticed by being the best in what you do. If you believe you can do a better job, then do it. Prove it with actions, not words.

Generally speaking, leadership positions are there for you to take. They're not, however, going to walk over to you and sit in your lap. I have grabbed all the leadership positions I've ever held. They didn't come to me. My experience makes me a firm believer in the idea that if you want something, you can have it. But you have to go out and get it.

A lot of people claim they're all with me on this idea but get stuck on the how. How do I just go out and grab what I want when what I want is a leadership job? It's simple, really. What you do is show what you are capable of doing, and people will notice. Leaders make the paths. They don't wait for someone to do it first then join in. Leaders set the example to follow. Complaining and making excuses isn't going to get you anywhere, and it's certainly not going to get you a leadership position.

If you desire success, copy what successful people do. Successful people don't whine and complain about everything. They make a plan and then execute it. I am a competitive person and need to be number one in everything I do, no matter what it is. Nobody remembers number two; number two is the first loser. Most pro football fans know the Indianapolis Colts won the Super Bowl in 2006, but who remembers who they played? And really, who cares? Nobody brags about making it to the Super Bowl. You brag only if you win.

It's the same with jobs. The problem is when people accept being passed over for a promotion, when people accept losing. It's just a game; it's just a job; it's no big deal. The people who accept defeat, who accept being passed over for promotions, are losers.

I know that sounds harsh. But if we want to be successful, we can't accept anything but success. I learned from all the people I met who were not successful, and I did the exact opposite of them. You can only judge results. You can't judge what people say they will do, but you can judge what they have already accomplished. The reason this is my first published article is simple. I needed first to achieve success in order to teach success.

The reason I am able to lead is simple: I have a great track record. People follow record breakers. This is why I strive to be number one in everything I do. You might not agree with my aggressive ways, but it doesn't matter, because I get results! You also will get results when you start to achieve in what you do. Get noticed for your results, not your talk.

Ace of Spades: Accountability

My final ace of success is the most important of all—the ace of spades, which represents accountability. A spade is a work tool used to turn earth. We can stand around and lean on it, or we can use it turn earth and weed our gardens. Either way, if we've got the spade, we need to be accountable for our work or lack of work. It's human nature for people to want credit for their accomplishments. It's also human nature for people not to want to be accountable for their mistakes. But I'm telling you, if you want to be successful, you have to be accountable.

Integrity means taking responsibility for your mistakes immediately. I can tell you from personal experience, life is a lot easier when you own up to your mistakes right away. I read a book once in which two men are talking, and one man says to the other, "If you kicked the person responsible for your problems, you wouldn't be able to sit for weeks." That story made me laugh because it is so true.

There were times in my life when I would blame my troubles and current situation on racism, my upbringing, my record, my lack of education, and so on, blah, blah, blah. When we're looking to keep the spotlight of responsibility off us, we can go on and on. I remember a time when I was afraid to have kids because I would hear so many people say they couldn't do this, that, or the other thing because they had kids. Now I realize that having children is a blessing, not an excuse to fail.

So often when I work with people, they say things like, "You don't understand; it's hard because I have children." Actually, I do understand. And I also understand that children are a reason to succeed, not to fail.

Remember this next time you're feeling sorry for yourself and blaming your lack of success on bearing extra burdens because you have children: Your children follow your lead. If you accept failure, they will too. If you complain about life and make excuses for your failure, they will too.

Accountability can be scary, because when you take responsibility, you're admitting fault. No one ever wants to take fault. No way, we say. It wasn't me; it was the one-armed man. Some people might blame failure at work on the fact that they don't like their boss. "It's not my attitude," they say, "it's just that my boss is a jerk." Or maybe they blame failure on a company's culture. "I'm not getting ahead here because people in this company are racist." I know because I used to think this way. Don't get me wrong. The world is full of jerk bosses and racist people, but neither needs to stand in the way of your success.

People often ask me my nationality. I very proudly say I am a Mexi-Can, not a Mexi-Can't. I look at myself as a successful man, and race has nothing to do with it. I actually heard someone say, "Those people have money because they are white." What? Does that mean that because I was blessed with a tan, I'm out of luck, that I should just pack up and go back to Mexico? Whoops. I forgot. I was born here. I don't have any place to go back to.

That kind of poisonous thinking is spread throughout our community. The point here is that if you are not successful, it might well be because you are lazy, not because you are Mexican. When I hear that garbage talk, that woe is me, the white people are holding us down, I tune it out. It shows low self-esteem, and it takes us off the hook. "We don't have to be responsible or accountable because the cards have been stacked against us." That's just wrong. Look. Racism is a problem in our country. I'm not denying that. But people of color can succeed. We need to stop blaming our failure on the color of our skin and start taking responsibility for our own lives.

Some people might say that I'm insensitive and don't understand the pressures facing people of color in our country. I have a ready response for that. I'm Mexican. I was poor and raised on welfare. I ran with a gang, went to prison, dropped out of school, and had no father to guide me. When I went to get a job, companies denied me because of my background. Adults treated me poorly when I was a kid. I was heavily in debt, and I used to live on credit cards. I've been robbed, and I've been fired. My house was fire-bombed. I was placed in protective custody. And yet, today, I am making it happen. Should I say more?

The list can go on forever. I remember the last time I was in jail. Ironically, it was the first time I was actually innocent. I took the fall for a friend. I remember I wasn't too disappointed because I was promised my job when I got out. Or so I thought. The company decided to let me go. I could have easily felt sorry for myself, knowing that there was nothing I could do from behind bars but wait until I got out to try and pick up the pieces. But the thing is, there was something I could do, and instead of feeling sorry for myself, I did what I could. Even though I no longer had a job to go back to, I did have some vacation money coming to me. So I started making business plans from behind bars. I knew that without a job, I needed a plan B.

One thing that kept me going was a cartoon I remembered depicting a pelican trying to swallow a frog back legs first, but the frog was using its front legs to choke the pelican. The caption read simply, "Never give up."

On the flip side of the cartoon was a passage that read:

Attitude, to me, is more important than facts. It is more important than the past, the education, the money, than circumstances, than failure, than successes, than what other people think or say or do. It is more important than appearance, giftedness, or skill. It will make or break a company . . . a church . . . a home. The remarkable thing is we have a choice every day regarding the attitude we will embrace for that day. We cannot change our past . . . we cannot change the fact that people will act in a certain way. We cannot change the inevitable. The only thing we can do is play on the one string we have, and that is our attitude. I am convinced that life is 10% what happens to me and 90% of how I react to it. And so it is with you . . . we are in charge of our attitudes.

I believe everything happens for a reason. There is no such thing as a coincidence. I have made many mistakes in my life, and I don't make excuses for them. I embrace them. They made me who I am today. I take responsibility for what I've done, and that includes the failures as well as the successes, the mistakes and the victories.

To achieve great success, you need to be accountable for everything that happens in your life, both good and bad. Learn from your failures and document your successes. Get ready for what you've been looking for—success. Success is that seemingly elusive thing that so many talk about, that everyone wants but only a few ever see. Be one of the few. Join me in the journey and forge your own successful walk through life.

I have much more to share, and I know you can benefit from my experience. A lot of my learning was gained the hard way, but there's no reason for you to make the same mistakes I did. Just follow the four aces of success, and you'll be sure to start living the life of your dreams.

I'm living proof that no matter where you start in life, you can finish on top. It all starts with a positive attitude and a willingness to stay away from losers. Or to put it more positively, you must have a willingness to associate with winners. Next, you have to be competitive and committed to doing what you need to do to succeed. And finally, you must be accountable, willing to accept responsibility for both your successes and mistakes. Put these four aces to work for you, and you'll be well along your road to success.

About the Author

Jose De La Torre, Jr., lives with his wife and son in Westchester, Illinois. He is a successful entrepreneur, author, speaker, and owner of SFE LLC. For more information, please visit www.oymuniversity.com.

Think It, Act It, Attract It

Daniel Lister

So there I was in 2004, in the midst of building my record empire. I knew what I wanted and exactly how I was going to get it, and I couldn't get there quickly enough. When I go, I go hard! Eating and sleeping were delays on my journey to success.

I awoke at 8 a.m., got to university to study for my audio engineering degree by 10, stayed in class until 2, went to the studio to make beats until 8, left the studio and went straight to my cousin Joel's house to make more beats until 2 a.m., headed home to make still more beats until 5 a.m., and then got to sleep before doing it all again. Some days I would go to class, then go straight to the studio and stay there all day, all evening, all night—right 'round until morning—and then go back to class. I believed I could train my body to operate on four hours of sleep.

I was all day every day, ain't no half steppin', no days off like

Ferris Bueller. I was in Ride or Die mode—and I nearly did die!

So there I was, in a hospital bed looking up at the ceiling, fighting for my life. I had been so *focused* on my goal and trying to achieve it that I had run my body and immune system into the ground. As a result I caught pneumonia, but not ordinary pneumonia. When this pneumonia came, it came hard.

All the top doctors from the hospital and other hospitals with all kinds of letters after their names tried to cure me with no success. They tried regular strength antibiotic tablets, medium strength, then maximum strength. When that didn't work, they tried pumping all strengths of antibiotics directly into my veins, and when that didn't work, they tried giving me a combination of the two—pills and IVs. Then finally a result: Not only did I have pneumonia, I also had swollen kidneys from all the drugs they had given me. After three and a half long weeks and all the effort put in by the top doctors in the hospital, my pneumonia was finally cured with homemade remedies by my Auntie Loraine!

The worst thing that happened to me didn't happen to my body, but to my mind. While in the hospital, I couldn't make any music, and I didn't listen to any either. I didn't read any of the industry magazines or check the websites; I had no contact with that life. Now you have to understand that before going into the hospital, music was my life. The only time I wasn't listening to some was when I was sleeping, and even then I would go to sleep with and wake up with music. I was so hooked that I was mad when I was making music because I couldn't listen to music!

But during my bout with pneumonia, all I did was stare at the lilac wall and the white ceiling. I was fine for two weeks, but at the end of the third, a strange thing started happening to me. I began to forget who I was. I was away from my previous life so long that everything I related to was a fading memory, the world as I had known it ceased to exist, and I felt like I was going insane. By the time I left the hospital, I was a different person, and I came home to someone else's life. I felt like a stranger in my own home. I would sit in silence, no TV, no music, just staring at the walls or looking around as people do when visiting someone's house for the first time. Eventually, over time, I learned to love all the things of my previous life again.

Throughout the whole ordeal, I learned a valuable lesson. *You are what you surround yourself with.* I had become a different person because I was immersed in a different lifestyle with different input. Therefore, I became a different person with different output.

The Law of Attraction

To succeed you must have crystal-clear goals. We wouldn't go through our front door and then decide our destination, so why do we go through life with no destination? You must write down your goals, dreams, and visions and look at them regularly, at least three times a day—once when you wake up, once at midday, and once just before you go to sleep—and you must visualize them and try to hold the vision as long as possible.

Looking at your goals regularly not only reminds you of where you're heading, but it also engages the reticular activating system, which is a function of the reticular formation within your brain. The reticular formation is connected to areas of your brain called the cerebral cortex, thalamus, and hypothalamus, all of which are responsible for functions like arousal, motivation, and consciousness.

The hypothalamus connects your nervous system to your endocrine system, which is a series of glands that regulate your body, especially your mood. The glands of the endocrine system have an energy field that is most commonly known as your chakras or your aura. So when you look at your goals regularly, not only does it physically prepare your body for success, but it also helps to tune you in to the frequency of success.

Your aura is just the frequency vibration of the energy your body is giving off. Everything vibrates and gives off energy. If you could tune in to that energy, you would find it has a color, a sound, a temperature, and other physical characteristics. In fact, there are cameras called aura cameras that can actually tune in to the frequency and take a picture of the color of your aura. Have you ever heard angry people say, "I saw red"? Well, red was the color they saw or felt that came along with that vibrational mood. It's what is known as bad vibes. "Vibes" is just short for vibrations. Have you ever walked into a room after an argument and just felt the tension or heard the saying "you could cut the tension with a knife"? Well, the people who were arguing were giving off such negative energy that they literally charged the atmosphere, and when you walked in, you felt that charge.

Just as you can give off a negative vibration, you can give off a positive one. After I've spoken, people have said things like, "The atmosphere was electric." Have you ever felt drawn to someone or got the feeling that someone is either successful or bound for success? Well, did you know that there is a success frequency? By inputting the right information, you can tune your body to the success frequency, give off successful vibes, and in turn attract success through the law of attraction. *Think it, act it, attract it.*

> *Success is not to be pursued; it is to be attracted by the*
> *person you become.*
> —Jim Rohn

The law of attraction states that "like attracts like." The reason it is important to visualize your goals and dreams is that "thoughts become things." The more vivid, energetic, and passionate you are about your dreams, the stronger the attraction and the faster and more likely they are to become reality.

Everything you see is made up of elements. Let's take your favorite sports car, for instance. Visualize it. Can you see it? Well, the actual car is made up of materials, including metal, wood, glass, and carbon fiber. All those materials are made up of elements, the simplest of which is the hydrogen atom. If you were to look further to the subatomic level, you would see protons and neutrons. If you could see further still, you would find quarks, bi-aps, and zeles (or zedes). If you kept going, you would eventually get to pure energy, the energy that makes up all things in existence. We'll just call this ALL energy. This ALL energy is the base of all things. Some people may call it the universe, some might call it God, but we will just call it ALL.

Thoughts have weight, shape, and form.
—Dr. Malachi Z. York-El

When you visualized your favorite sports car, did it exist? Of course it did! That thought or vision had a weight, shape, and form and was made up of ALL energy, the same as the physical car. If you held that vision long enough, and it was vivid and energetic enough, through the law of attraction the ALL energy in your vision would attract the ALL energy in the physical car. Have you ever been talking about someone and suddenly he or she just turns up? Or thinking of someone and out of the blue he or she just calls you? That's the law of attraction. You visualized it into existence. And you can do that with your dreams. Of course, the bigger the dream, the stronger the vision needs to be.

Get Your Mind Right

Change will not come if we wait for some other person or some other time. We are the ones we've been waiting for. We are the change that we seek.
—Barack Obama

They say you are what you eat. It is also true that you are what you think. Everything in your life is a result of the decisions you made with your thought patterns and thought processes. Nine out of ten decisions are made by the subconscious mind, which is already preprogrammed, meaning that the majority of outcomes in your life are already predecided. If you're happy with your life, then great. But if you're not happy with your life, then things need to change. Jim Rohn said, "In order for things to change, first you must change." Albert Einstein said, "The height of insanity is to do the same thing over and over again and expect different results."

To change, you must reprogram your subconscious. Have you ever said something you didn't mean to say that just slipped out? Or have you ever done something that just came out of nowhere? That was your subconscious coming through with what you really thought and felt. Have you ever been in front of opportunity, not recognized it, and then five minutes later thought, "Damn, I should have approached that prospect," or "Damn, I should have dropped that line and then asked for her phone number!" Well, that was because your subconscious wasn't aligned with your goals, dreams, and desires. Once it is, your subconscious will arrange your every thought, word, and action in line with your vision, and success will be effortless.

So how do you reprogram your subconscious for success?

Every second of every minute of your life you are programming yourself with your senses, so you must immerse yourself in successful people, places, and things. Contrast that with what most people program themselves with—television programs! Your subconscious doesn't know the difference between what is real and what isn't. Have you ever watched a scary movie and jumped, felt your heart skip a beat, or even started sweating? Did your body know the movie wasn't real?

There's a strange thing that happens to the mind when you

think the word "I." When you're watching the scary movie, and the cheerleader runs up the stairs to hide in the dead-end closet instead of running to the gun cabinet, and you think *I wouldn't have gone up there,* your subconscious automatically accepts it as reality because you used the word "I." When you watch your favorite soap and so-and-so's business fails, what's-her-name's relationship fails, and what's-his-face gets knocked back for trying, your subconscious accepts that as reality and forms your belief system about businesses, relationships, and trying new things.

On the other hand, have you ever watched an inspirational film like *The Pursuit of Happiness*? How did you feel after it? What was your perspective on life? After watching it, did you feel like anything was possible? The film programmed your subconscious and changed your belief system, and then you believed anything was possible. And guess what? Whether you think you can or you think you can't, either way you're right! Your belief system determines your actions.

Prior to 1954, people believed it was impossible to run a mile in under four minutes. Doctors said that if a man attempted it, his lungs would explode. In 1954, Roger Bannister ran the first four-minute mile. That year more than two hundred people ran the mile in under four minutes. Now the standard for middle-distance runners is the four-minute mile. Schoolchildren are doing it, people in their forties are doing it, people are running two four-minute miles back to back. What happened? Did the mile get shorter? Did four minutes suddenly become longer? No! The only thing that changed was peoples' belief systems. Once they saw it done, they believed they could do it, which affected their actions, which in turn affected their results.

Dreams are hopeless aspiration in hopes of coming true; believe in yourself—the rest is up to me and you.
—Lisa "Left Eye" Lopez

Surrounding yourself with success leads to a successful belief system, which in turn leads to successful actions that produce successful results. To be successful, you must immerse yourself in success and be 100 percent committed to your goals, dreams, desires, and vision. You can't be half in and half out because no one wins the race by running halfway.

Stay focused!

About the Author

Daniel "Focus" Lister is a highly motivated individual and an electrifying, dynamic, and thought-provoking speaker. He travels up and down the length and breadth of the UK teaching young people in a way they can relate to how to go from negative to positive through personal development and entrepreneurialism. He speaks to all ages, but his passion is helping young people.

Lister is also a coach, teacher, and mentor. He runs courses and workshops and still finds time to be a successful businessman and entrepreneur. Daniel is a faculty member and a proud student of Success University. He also does presentations for Success University throughout the UK.

For more information or to book Daniel, contact www.MrDLister. com or Daniel@MrDLister.com. For more about Success University, go to www.GetFocused.SuccessUniversity.com/new.

Create Your Amazing Life

Elaine Powell

I was born in London in 1967. My father, Calbert, emigrated from Jamaica in 1959, and my mother, Kay, from St. Lucia when she was sixteen. Both bore an adventurous and courageous spirit that they used in search of a better and more fulfilling life. I was the youngest of three children and as such was carefree and mischievous. I lived quite a sheltered upbringing, apart from my parents divorcing when I was ten. I left school well educated, with good qualifications, but I had no interest in pursuing academia.

In my twenties I fell deeply in love, and for seven years my partner was the center of my life. When this relationship ended, all I had left was work and an empty space. I had spent so much time loving, caring for, and putting all my energies into my partner that I had neglected one of the most important things: to focus on myself. I spiraled downward into clubbing, drinking, smoking, depression, and a cycle of what I call "PMS" (Poor Me Syndrome). I played out my groundhog day repeatedly, day after day, and sank deeper into depression.

I did not have a plan for my life, so life decided that, in the absence of my input, it would take me on whatever journey it dictated. I was twenty-eight years old, had a minimal understanding of myself, no vision, no real purpose. I was an empty vessel, drifting along, just existing. I was searching. For what, I did not know. All I knew was that this feeling was deep within, and I couldn't find the words to express it.

I was searching, and when God came along to fill that vast void inside me, I felt like I was home. A lot of people ask me whether I was in a low state when I found God, and I have to answer "yes." This seems to be true for a lot of people. I've often asked myself why this is, wondering whether it's because when we're feeling like we hit rock bottom that we become more humble and willing to ask for help, or whether we simply begin to ask ourselves fundamental questions about life. In Matthew 7:7, Jesus says, "Ask and it will be given to you; seek and you will find; knock and the door will be opened to you." Could it be that simple? Yes. Getting help from God is as simple as putting a plug into a socket and receiving a supply of electricity.

Finding God has been a major life-transforming experience. I call it My Awakening. I began to ask long-overdue questions: Who is God? Why is the world the way it is? Why am I here? God answered by sending me a teacher, a wonderful lady who sat patiently with me for a year. We diligently went through the Bible finding the answers to my questions. Although at the time I did not fully believe in God, I was willing to at least try to believe.

The more questions I asked, the more answers I received. I went inside myself to what I call my internal garden and started to pull up all the weeds, stones, and garbage that had accumulated over the years and overshadowed the beautiful flower underneath. I believe that being honest with and about yourself is one of the best things you can do. If more than two people say the same thing about you, you need to listen. There is a saying that runs, "If people keep on calling you a donkey, you better check to see if you have hooves." Yes, facing your shortcomings may hurt at first, but what will hurt more is the impact certain behaviors may have on your life and those around you.

In the film *The Matrix*, Neo is given the choice between "the red pill of enlightenment" or "the blue pill of ignorance." I had no choice but to take the red pill. I became like a child again, excited about life and full of questions. I now believe that it is our destiny to find our purpose and to live our lives to their full potential, to be the best we can in all we do. Until then, we are continually restless within. I continued to be restless, although I was on the road to having a greater understanding of myself.

I had been working within the legal establishment for twelve years. The money was good, but fulfillment was not forthcoming. I decided to ask myself what I really wanted to do, and I found that I truly yearned to work with children. So I left my job and began working in a secure establishment for boys aged ten to seventeen years with behavioral and emotional difficulties. Some of these young people were sentenced or awaiting trial, and others were there for welfare reasons, having become involved in drugs, sexual assaults, pedophilia and other antisocial or criminal behaviors.

I worked extensively with these young people using cognitive learning therapy, changing their behavior using positive reinforcement. I saw great improvements in their actions when they were given guidance, positive attention, and a behavioral plan to follow. I achieved a great sense of fulfillment working with young people, and I worked within the establishment for five years. It was at this point that I made another life-changing decision.

I had become somewhat bemused about the way our society

stipulated that we should work hard until sixty-five and only then retire and have free time. I decided to have free time now. Why wait? My plan was to go traveling around the world for a year. Well, I was amazed by how many people could not understand why I wanted to do this. People told me I'd be away too long, reminded me that I have a house, or worried that I was a single female traveling alone. Many people tried to talk me out of going. I was glad I listened to my internal guide and didn't rely on my other senses because I might have talked myself out of going. They say you can use your five senses to take you to the end of the road, but your sixth sense knows what's around the corner. Listening to my internal spiritual guide would fare me well while traveling.

Thailand was the beginning of my adventure and proved to be my base while in Asia. I travelled to Cambodia, Vietnam, Laos, and then back into Thailand. Many travelers I encountered spoke about India, and I realized I was very near it and so off I sallied. While in India, I was achingly close to Nepal, so off I ventured. Are you seeing the pattern here? Naturally, being in the neighborhood, I had to saunter into the land that time forgot, Tibet.

After five weeks, I returned to India, where I experienced my biggest culture shock. What a land of contradictions, poverty vs. wealth, spirituality vs. materialism, cleanliness vs. dirtiness, magnificent forts vs. a blanket sheltering a family of five who lived and cooked on the main street of Jaipur. I stayed for a challenging month and then returned to Thailand. The remainder of the year, I traveled to Malaysia, Singapore, Indonesia, Australia, New Zealand, Chile, Argentina, Bolivia, Peru, Brazil, and Spain.

I compare all these countries to a humongous meal consisting of eighteen starters. Some were very good, some should be taken off the menu forever, and some I ordered as main courses, savoring them before consuming them with gratification.

The feeling of freedom was amazing. I was in full charge of where I went and when I went. Every day was filled with new sights, sounds, experiences, and encounters. I was silenced by the beauty of the landscape, met some phenomenal charismatic people, and delighted in tantalizing cultures. I threw myself into living life to the fullest, and in doing so became a master scuba diver, went on safaris, and sky dived, to name just a few exploits. I visited majestic Mount Everest, the tantalizing Taj Mahal, the astounding Angkor Wat, the mesmerizing Machu Picchu, and I even reveled at Rio de Janeiro carnival.

Upon returning to London, one year later, somewhat burnt out from extensive traveling and exposure to so many experiences, I was amazed by how many people appeared to be walking around like zombies, with no eye contact, no smiles, completely lacking energy and gusto for life. Perhaps they were not fulfilled in their jobs, were living a life of mediocrity, or had given up on their dreams and aspirations.

I eventually returned to work, but after six months, I stood in my garden and cried. I cried that the same fate might await me. I cried that I had just had a year of freedom, being my own boss, and now somebody else was my boss once again. This was when I decided to make that change.

They say you get exactly what you focus on. Before I traveled, my focus had been on a better job and security. Now my focus was on being my own boss, great relationships, financial freedom, and more free time. I truly believe when the mind and emotions interplay, nothing can stop them. I said, "I can't do this anymore" and life said, "Your wish is my command." When we want something passionately enough, we transmit our desire into the universe, and we get responses back.

Upon reflection, I have seen that my past was littered with clues of where I was heading. At school, I wanted to be a teacher. Now I teach others how to believe in themselves and their dreams. In searching, I found God, and in doing so, found myself. I traveled to countries and environments that helped expand my mind and vision, and I experienced freedom. Now I am an inspirational speaker and help others have the courage to be free, pursue their dreams, and live an amazing life. I believe I have been successful in finding the right road to fulfill my dreams and purpose, so below I share with you some points that have helped me along the way, and I pray that they will help you create your amazing life.

Commit to Your Dreams and Purpose

When Martin Luther King, Jr., sought to energize the civil rights movement in the United States, he said, "I have a dream." He understood that the dream is where it starts. You have to know where you're going in order to get there. Spend some quality quiet time asking yourself a few poignant questions. *What is my purpose? What do I love to do and how do I get paid to do it? What do I want to do with my life and why aren't I doing it? How can I help others?* If you don't ask the right questions, you won't get the right answers.

Les Brown said, "Don't worry about how you're going to do it; how is none of your business." As you start to take action in your life, you will meet people (I call them angels) who will help take you to the next level, and opportunities will present themselves to you. When you set your mind and spirit to achieve, everything comes into play to make it happen. Be committed to and passionate about reaching your dreams.

Discover Your Why

Finding out your Why is extremely important. Your Why, essentially, is your purpose. Your Why could be that you want to leave a legacy for your children, or you want to help other people and therefore need more free time. Your Why is unique to you and will help you keep focused when times are difficult. Write it out and place it where you can read it daily.

Write Out Your Life Plan, Read It Daily, and Take Action

A Yale University study found that 3 percent of people who had written down their goals were worth more twenty years later than the other 97 percent, who did not write down their goals, combined. When you want to create a business, one of the first things you have to do is write out a business plan. How much more important is our life compared with a business plan? How many of us can say, "Yes, I have mapped out a plan for my life"?

Write down your goals for where you want your life to be in one, two, five, ten, twenty, and fifty years. Now work backwards and clearly state the actions needed to reach your goals. Write out ten goals afresh every single day for twenty-one days for this to become a habit and watch the amazing results surface. Ask yourself daily, "what did I do today to get closer to my dream and what can I do tomorrow?"

"The hierarchy of your values determines how you perceive and act upon the world and therefore your destiny," said Dr. John F. Demartini. Your goals must be congruent with your values. Set priorities and focus on the task of highest value first. Concentrate single-mindedly on it until finished. Continually ask yourself, "what is the most valuable use of my time" and delegate everything else.

Strengthen Your Faith and Belief

All things are possible. You alone are able to set limits for yourself and are capable of realizing your success. Learn to listen to your intuition, which is God trying to give you guidance. All things inspired come from God. It is far better to have God on your side than not to have him involved at all. Therefore, I suggest that you put all things in prayer. If you open your heart to God, you will be amazed how people and doors open in your life to make all things possible.

So start believing in yourself. Remind yourself every day that you are amazing and that you were put on this earth with a purpose to fulfill.

> *Trust in the Lord, with all your heart, and do not lean on your*
> *own understanding. Seek His will in all you do and*
> *He will direct your path.*
> —Proverbs 3:5-6.

Remember that Words Are Powerful

Everything you have or don't have in your life is a result of the words that you spoke into your life in the past. If people understood how powerful their words were, they would possibly be too scared to say anything. When we release words, everything lines up with what we say to bring it about. It is while we are waiting for the manifestation that we may cancel out the gift by speaking negative words. As we learn from Proverbs (18:21), "The tongue has the power of life and death."

Write and memorize positive affirmations about yourself and your life. Proclaim these affirmations several times throughout the day, while believing in yourself and in your mission.

Use Your Mind Positively

We are the problem and the solution. It is said that we have sixty thousand thoughts a day. What a lot of chatter. I began to listen to this internal chatter and realized that a large chunk of it was negative, nonproductive, and a waste. I commenced the slow process of learning to be in control of my thoughts. When negative, nonproductive thoughts crept in, I thought of something positive, or I told myself this wasn't helping me and immediately stopped that thought.

You become and attract what you think about most in your life. You attract the most dominant thoughts, whether they are conscious or unconscious, so focus with a lot of passion on positive things that you want to happen.

You are what you put into yourself. Become an avid reader of books that will develop you and put you ahead of the crowd. Just as there are laws of nature and science, there are laws to becoming successful. Learn those laws and develop the mindset of a winner. Don't be limited by limited thinking.

See Failure for What It Really Is

Failure is simply learning how to do it more intelligently next time. It is necessary to have courage, take risks, and stop living small. Failure is part of the learning process, and life is a continual test. If you haven't already, you must take on this mindset and mentality. Failure is just a learning opportunity. Face your fears head on and watch yourself grow. Self-mastery is not being swayed by events, either positive or negative; just remain focused.

Take Time to Be Grateful

Spend ten minutes a day recognizing your goodness and giving thanks. Giving thanks for the good things in life is an essential part of receiving more of those things in return. Learn to be silent, to be an open doorway for things to positively enter your mind and your life. Sit in a quiet place and picture being in a calm place. Take deep breaths and think, feel, and visualize what it will feel like to reach your dreams and the person you must become to achieve them.

I pray that you seek courage to birth your dreams, seek action to apply them, and seek strength to pursue them to the end.

I know you will do great, because you are truly amazing!

God bless you.

About the Author

Elaine Powell is an inspirational speaker, a member of Toastmasters, and a certified practitioner of Neuro-Linguistic Programming (NLP). Elaine is dedicated to deliver training programs that improve team and individual productivity and growth. She has achieved phenomenal results in helping people to break the bondage of any limited thinking and reach for their true potential. Elaine is also a member of and presents for Success University. She has travelled to more than forty countries worldwide. During a one-year expedition around the world in 2005, she traveled to a staggering eighteen countries. This epic journey is told in her forthcoming book *Amazing World, Amazing People.*

Elaine became a born-again Christian in 2004. One of her visions in life is to help inspire people spiritually, mentally, and emotionally to live full and abundant lives. Her special strength lies in her courage and willingness to step outside her comfort zone to fulfill her purpose and her dedication to help others do the same. For more information on Elaine, please visit www.elainepowell.com or contact her at ep@elainepowell.com.

Evolutionary Psychology

Nik Halik

With everything we do in our lives, we need to resonate in harmonic vibration with our core beliefs and values, so that we can achieve what we desire. As I travel the globe, I often get asked about the secrets of success and financial prosperity. People want to know how I can assist them in discovering financial freedom. My response is that I can educate them with an array of wealth pillars, but this only composes about 1 percent of the equation. Ninety nine percent is the psychological attribute. It's a way of freedom. Quite simply, it's about unlocking your potential. I was born rich in human potential. I was certainly not born into wealth. I had to discover the formula to wealth prosperity on my own by embracing myriad strategies. My personal goal each year is to blast off on a new paradigm and continually be in the orbit of the most influential minds on the planet. Hence the evolution of the mind that is paramount here.

Some indigenous Indians in the Amazon have lived to a phenomenal age. Some have been reported to be well into their hundreds, even as old as 150. Why do they live so long? My belief is that they have never been programmed to die at seventy or eighty the way that people in Western society have been. Programming is a powerful and restrictive force in our lives. We've been hardwired to think in certain ways and to follow patterns set by the system. This works against our own individuality and limits what we can achieve. It certainly restricts us from achieving our dreams. What we all need to do is delete our old programming.

The Parthenon has stood for thousands of years because it has a strong foundation and a structure of supportive pillars. The foundation of it is equivalent to your belief system and mindset. If your initial foundation is contaminated, you're attempting to build a financial future on quicksand. This dream-drowning sand will permeate your life if left unchecked.

If you want to erect a skyscraper, you must ensure that your mindset and foundations are solid. Your goal is to build a solid base on which to erect financial pillars. Most people who've been to Italy have been to Pisa, a city in Tuscany, to visit a famous leaning tower. Why is it called the Leaning Tower of Pisa? Most people think the answer is because of its defective structural engineering. The truth is that the soil in its base was contaminated with unstable subsoil that allowed the foundation to shift direction. Hence, the design was flawed from the beginning. For hundreds of years, in an effort to compensate for the tilt, engineers built higher-angled floors with one side taller than the other to allow the tower to lean in the other direction. A multinational task force of engineers, mathematicians, and historians over the past eight hundred years were assigned to save it from collapsing. What they all failed to realize was the importance of the subsoil foundation in the first place. What does this metaphor share with the foundation of our lives?

The Leaning Tower of Pisa remains a marvel, but you don't want to build your financial future on shaky foundations. You need to have a solid blueprint and firm foundations as early as possible to avoid financial cancer and to ensure financial prosperity. You need an antivirus protection program for the mind. Unfortunately, many of us fail to believe in ourselves and in our own ability to think. We doubt our ability to create, and our ability to achieve. If we don't believe in ourselves, we lack accountability.

A desert becomes a forest with the right gardener. Imagine a tree of life. The tree of life is an important symbol in nearly every culture, with its branches reaching into the sky, and its roots growing deep into the soil of the earth. An eternal tree of life bears fruit. In life, our fruits are the equivalent of our manifested results. So, what does humanity tend to do? Most people focus too much attention on the fruits, the monetary results. But the seeds and the roots create the ripeness of those fruits. It's what's under the ground that is the secret garden, and the nurturing of the soil creates what is above the ground. This hidden gem is the invisible component that manifests the visible results in your life. What you cannot see in this world is far more powerful than anything that you can see. This garden analogy proves to be the fertile reasoning in giving birth to some of life's most valuable lessons. Just as seeds in a garden require sun, water, and soil to thrive, the seeds of positive thought require adequate nurturing in the form of discipline and a belief system. By transforming the composition of the fruits, you first have to transform the roots. If you want to change the visible, you must first change the invisible.

We need to define our "why" in life, which provides our sense of purpose. This act stimulates our brain's neural networking and is a modeling process that provides the reasoning and catalyst for change. When we have a powerful vision, we bend the universe to our will. An individual without a why is a ship without a rudder. No matter how hard you attempt to sail the rudderless ship, it goes nowhere. It just churns water, totally ineffectively. Once we formulate our why, every action in our lives takes on a more definite meaning. From that moment forward, every action etched in our minds manifests itself in reality toward our goals. I was very fortunate to experience this paradigm shift of thinking, even though at the time I didn't even know what a paradigm was.

If you could hear somebody read the eulogy of your life upon your passing, what would you like to hear? A eulogy personalized about your life could be the toughest speech you'd ever be forced to listen to. What would the overall theme convey? What legacy would you leave behind that would enable others to find strength? Most people have only a vague idea about what they want to do, and no real direction in their lives. This is when the reading of the eulogy takes a dramatic turn.

Would you ask for one more chance and more time to prove yourself? What would you do differently if you had more time? What are some tasks you would definitely commit to if you were granted more time? What would you be willing to do, just for another hour of life, another day, or perhaps even an extra year? Assuming you have the life you desire from this moment on, what will your eulogy say about your life?

Your goal needs to be something tangible, that is, real or physical. Also, if your goals do not inspire you, you will not be driven to achieve them. For every goal and ambition, you need to ask yourself the following question: *Is what I'm doing right now moving me toward or away from my goals?* By being definite, you can take daily stock of your life. Ask yourself, *Have I discovered something new?* You'll notice that I use the word "discover" quite often. I'm careful not to use the word "learn." I feel the word is too closely associated with the academic system and can be considered negative by many people. The schooling system is such an irrelevant institution in its current format. "Learn" is not a word I want to perpetuate here.

Discovery is all about empowerment and the DNA of our soul. The soul of your DNA is the composition of your dreams, destiny lived, conscious and unconscious. It is made of your past, your successes, and especially your failures. This discovery phase reinforces the need to harness new energies and opportunities in our lives—just like the exploration of new frontiers in space.

Daily life should always consist of embracing new distinctions of change and an optimized set of higher values. This process validates your thinking faculty. Most people who are trapped with an institutionalized mindset fail to think for themselves. They've lost their ability to think and have simply become a warehouse of facts. I personally believe that many institutionalized people are lucky enough to think twice a year. In many cases, people tend to think only in times of emergency. In normal life, they haven't raised their level of awareness to what's around them. They have become slaves to a program of conventional thought installed from birth, slaves to something called the System.

This System of thought has programmed their mindset. Their free thought has been commandeered to the extent that they are no longer able to ask probing questions or challenge the status quo. Programming occurs everywhere—from the moment we go to school and when we join the workforce. Switch on the news, or pick up a newspaper, and you'll see the parameters of the System set by those who rule the System. Most people don't challenge themselves enough to see the System for what it is. Unfortunately, most of humanity has been programmed to have one job or source of income. Why? It serves the System. What better way for the shepherd, the System, to control and sedate the flock?

Having one source of income and servicing your life with after-tax dollars is a sure-fire recipe for being dead broke. Now combine this thought with the fact that you were purposely denied financial education while at school in order to keep you financially ignorant.

Think about it: Were you ever educated about money at school? The result is that up to 95 percent of the working population works by necessity, doing whatever it takes to survive. Individuals across the globe are disconnected and remain subservient to the System.

When you look at the morning commute to get to work, most individuals are grinding away out of the necessity to do so. *The reality is you're working hard enough at work so you don't get sacked, while the employer pays you just enough so you don't quit.* A well-worn path isn't necessarily the right path to take in life. Humanity has been programmed to negate inner feelings and to work for the System.

The System reprimands dreamers. When you speak to kids, they have the most vivid dreams. They want to see the world, become firefighters, or travel to the moon. Why is it that in adult life, we no longer have those dreams, or we block ourselves from achieving those childhood dreams? The short answer is that we have allowed the System to institutionalize our mindset and take hold of us, hence making us servants of that System, as opposed to making the System our servant. We must become architects of our own lives, lighthouses of influence, illuminating our family and friends. This System was never designed for us or to look after us. It was designed to maintain the status quo and strengthen the institutional financial power brokers. Workers are always sent the bill and pay for everything. If there is some kind of disaster, we pay for it. The System is designed to spit out just enough cash to keep us just above what is regarded as the revolution level, where you are not out in the street burning and tearing the System apart.

In fact people who wear suits might get disgruntled with me for making this observation, but why else besides necessity would a man wear something as restrictive as a tie? It's a piece of cloth strung around your neck. It's a badge of the System. Of course, there may be people who wear ties because they like them, or because they're going to functions, or they want to fit in, but who would wear a suit and tie to work if they didn't have to? All these office workers wearing suits and ties—do they wear them by choice or by necessity? And there are the self-employed business owners who think they are not ruled by necessity, that they run their own businesses. When you take a closer look, though, you see that most self-employed people have purchased a job and become a slave to it. They just get to pay themselves last. Most self-employed people work *in* the job rather than *on* it. Working in the job means that your business relies on your physical presence to be able to generate cash flow. Most people working in their own business simply have bought themselves a job, work longer hours, carry all the responsibility, and pay themselves last.

I have utilized the opportunities given to me in my life and have strived to build the pillars of spiritual, psychological, physical, and monetary health on a solid foundation. Much of life is about a mindset. We all choose who we are and what we represent. It's an old saying, but it's true: "You are who you associate with." As a young man, attempting to find my path in the world, I always networked with individuals or groups who were transmitting a frequency of greater wisdom. I aspired to embrace their mindset. I believe that you either choose to walk through a new door of enlightenment or that door will be closed to you for the rest of your life. Unless you experience change and adopt higher values, the System will dominate your life.

I'll give you an example. If you go to your local railway station and board a morning train to the city, more often than not, you'll sit next to people who are expressionless or glum. But if you engage them in a conversation about their favorite hobbies, I bet they'll glow. Life will come into their faces. They will suddenly feel happy and animated. Their hobbies are what provide the exuberance in their lives. My question is, *Why can't people pursue their hobbies, do what makes them happy, all the time? Why don't their hobbies become their jobs?* Why not make investing your perpetual hobby once you've acquired the necessary financial skills?

Napoleon Hill, in his book *Think and Grow Rich,* said, "Action is the real measure of intelligence." Thomas Huxley, in *Aphorisms and Reflections,* said, "The great end of life is not knowledge but action." How can you act? Ask yourself these questions: *What thinking can I take on board to manifest the changes in my life? What can I do right now to change the path of my life? How can I challenge the status quo to take on new challenges? How can I generate more cash flow?*

An interesting facet of change is that it must encompass positive language patterns. The words "one day," "try," "wish," "hope," and "can't" are by far the most disempowering words we are guilty of using in our vocabulary. In relation to the "one day" statement, Confucius said, "Man shoot at nothing, sure to hit it." Think about this: If you are not aiming at anything in particular, you will have amazing accuracy at achieving it. By remaining date-specific and endorsing positive language patterns, we maintain accountability for our thoughts and actions. "Wish" and "hope" are words resonating in a negative vibration. Why wish or hope when you can strive for and create actionable steps to achieve success? The word "try" is essentially a failure disease. There is no such thing as try. We either make the conscious decision to do something or simply choose not to. *The Empire Strikes Back* (1980) contains a memorable line relating to the negative language of *trying.* This particular scene takes place in the swampland of the planet Dagobah, where a young Luke Skywalker, whose X-Wing Fighter is stuck in the swamp, is studying the Force under the training of Jedi Master Yoda.

> **Jedi Master Yoda:** "For my ally is the Force, and a powerful ally it is. Life creates it, makes it grow. Its energy surrounds us and binds us. Luminous beings are we, not this crude matter. You must feel the Force around you."
>
> **Luke Skywalker:** "All right, I'll give it a try."

Jedi Master Yoda: "No. Try not. Do or do not. There is no try."
Using the Force, Yoda effortlessly frees the X-Wing spacecraft
from the swamp.
Luke Skywalker: "I don't, . . . I don't believe it."
Jedi Master Yoda: "That is why you fail."

By using a filtering process, we can also start to set the parameters
for whom we invite into our lives. You can highlight whom you
desire to associate with. If people are negative, you can simply
avoid them. Associate with individuals who enlighten you. This
principle is similar to a car's filtering system. What does it do? It
removes impurities. The human mind is the world's largest filtering
device. We all have negative people in our lives, those who hold us
back or who frustrate us. Negative friends will never want you to
change. They want to hold you back where they are. Misery requires
company. Never allow their misery to engulf your life. Your choice
is to avoid those people and become a beacon of light for others to
follow. By nurturing weary souls searching for a lighthouse, you
will keep them from crashing against the rocky shores. You can
illuminate, enlighten, and enroll them in your dream.

It all begins with a belief system and a readiness to change. Unless
a student is ready, the teacher will never arrive. For most people, the
path to discovery and answers is already there. It's just a matter of
defining where that path is and how to follow it. We just need to
vaccinate ourselves against excusitis. Everyone has their pot of gold
or preferred choice of destination—what they aspire to accomplish
in life. It's a matter of finding it. We need to make the paths so vivid
that we can find them.

Unfortunately, most people live in a dim world. A pot of gold
may be just a few meters away, yet if your pot of gold is dim,
there's no way you'll find it. How do you light up your path? The
simple answer is by undergoing a metamorphosis. I wouldn't say
you need to have a light bulb moment; rather, you need to have
halogen moments of certainty. Once you have certainty, you begin

to accept more. Certainty removes fear. What do most people fear in life? They fear the unknown. How do you achieve certainty? By being definitive in everything you do in life. By defining your why and doing whatever it takes to achieve that why. That phrase "whatever it takes" is paramount here. You really do need to give all your mental energy to making this change. Every day people should ask themselves the following: *When was the last time I did something for the very first time? When was the last time I viewed a new vantage point in life?* If you think about that question carefully, you'll probably find that you've done the same thing over and over again. That is called the law of diminishing intent. It's doing the same thing over and over again but expecting a different outcome. If we're not willing to embrace new thoughts and experiences, we're effectively procrastinating.

Procrastination is a fear fertilizer. By fertilizing our fears and negativity, we proceed to justify why we've chosen not to change. We have a choice to alter our state of mind or to stay idle. In life, nothing around us stays the same. If we don't progress, we naturally regress. My suggestion is to list all the negative aspects of your life on one board. On a different board, list all the positive aspects of your life. Take stock of your life—spiritually, emotionally, physically, and monetarily. As an international wealth strategist and educator, whenever I take someone on as a client, I always insist that they encourage, enlighten, and nurture someone else to join them on their journey. *Kaizen* is a Japanese word that means a continuous and incremental improvement of a person's life. Kaizen involves taking small action steps over time to solve problems. The beauty of this approach lies in its simplicity. You begin something that initially seems daunting, but the small easy step helps you bypass the feelings of fear. If we procrastinate, we fertilize more fear. If we commit ourselves to the successful completion of a task, then we personify excellence. By simply introducing another small step and another, we jettison the confines of our comfort zone and relish in the power of self-examination.

In a 1960s London musical named *Time*, Sir Laurence Olivier played the character of the Time Lord. I was given the soundtrack of this famous excerpt ten years ago and forever absorbed every magical word. The premise is that we all possess a powerful key for the application of change in our lives:

Stand before me on the sign of infinity, all you of the earth. With the granting of the law of provination comes the application of change. I will give you the key. And with this knowledge, please realise, comes the responsibility of sharing it. I will show you the way. It's very simple. Throughout the universe there is order. In the movement of the planets, in nature and in the functioning of the human mind. A mind that is in its natural state of order is in harmony with the universe and such a mind is timeless. Your life is an expression of your mind. You are the creator of your own universe—for as a human being, you are free to will whatever state of being you desire through the use of your thoughts and words. There is great power there. It can be a blessing or a curse—it's entirely up to you. For the quality of your life is brought about by the quality of your thinking—think about that. Thoughts produce actions—look at what you're thinking. See the pettiness and the envy and the greed and the fear and all the other attitudes that cause you pain and discomfort. Realise that the one thing you have absolute control over is your attitude. See the effect that it has on those around you. For each life is linked to all life, and your words carry with them chain reactions like a stone that is thrown into a pond. If your thinking is in order, your words will flow directly from the heart, creating ripples of love. If you truly want to change your world, my friends, you must change your thinking. Reason is your greatest tool, it creates an atmosphere of understanding, which leads to caring, which is love. Choose your words with care. Go forth . . . with love.

Most people refuse to confront their own lives, probably because they're intimidated by what they'll find out. We don't have to accept our environment. These days the Internet has connected the world. We're more global, but unfortunately, our societies have grown more disconnected. Now computer games and video games trap our youth and leave them comatose in the confines of their home, removing them from their families and from the world around them. Once, people walked around their communities, their towns, their countries. Now everyone drives. The motorways are clogged with disconnected people. Communication used to be face to face. Now people exist on cell phones and in Internet chat rooms. When people undertake a serious appraisal of their lives, they should approach it with an honest and transparent perspective. We want to reflect on our lives and respect ourselves. We want to reflect positively on the mosaic of different cultural experiences in our lives. For me, it was the kaleidoscope of different adventures. For you, it could be whatever you desire, whatever response makes you passionate about your why.

At many wealth conferences across the globe, I often ask people a specific question that intrigues me because of the multiple complexities of responses. I ask them, "Where is the richest place in the world?" Most people incorrectly say Dubai, the United States, Saudi Arabia . . . . What do you think my response to them is? "The richest place in the world is the graveyard of all the dreams that were never fulfilled. In life we have to fight for our dreams; otherwise, unfulfilled dreams have a habit of haunting us for the rest of our lives."

Carpe diem: seize the day. The definition of this concept was poignantly illustrated in a magical scene in Peter Weir's movie *Dead Poets Society*. The setting is in 1959, at the Welton Academy in Vermont. Welton was an old-fashioned but well-respected private school, where education was preached in a rigorous academic arena combined with the shaping of traditionalist ideals. In this scene, the school walls are lined with class pictures dating back into the 1800s. School trophies of every description fill trophy cases and shelves. John Keating, the teacher who is the students' inspiration and who will make their lives extraordinary, played by Robin Williams, faces the class.

Keating: "Gather ye rosebuds while ye may. The Latin term for that sentiment is *carpe diem.* Anyone know what that means?"

Meeks: "Carpe diem . . . seize the day."

Keating: "Seize the day while you're young. See that you make use of your time. Why does the poet write these lines?"

A student: "Because he's in a hurry?"

Keating: 'Because we're food for worms, lads! Because we're only going to experience a limited number of springs, summers, and falls. One day, hard as it is to believe, each and every one of us is going to stop breathing, turn cold, and die! Stand up and peruse the faces of the boys who attended this school sixty or seventy years ago. Don't be timid. Go look at them."

The boys get up and go over to the class pictures that line the walls. Faces of young men stare at them from out of the past.

Keating: "They're not that different than any of you, are they? There's hope in their eyes, just like in yours. They believe themselves destined for wonderful things, just like many of you. Well, where are those smiles now, boys? What of that hope?"

The boys are staring at the pictures, sobered by what Keating is saying.

Keating: "Did most of them not wait until it was too late before making their lives into even one iota of what they were capable? In chasing the almighty deity of success, did they not squander their boyhood dreams? Most of those gentlemen are fertilizing daffodils! However, if you get very close, boys, you can hear them whisper. Go ahead, lean in, hear it?

(Loud whisper) "Carpe diem, lads. Seize the day. Make your lives extraordinary."

About the Author

Nik Halik is the founder and CEO of Financial Freedom Institute and Money Masters Global and co-founder of The Intelligence Group of companies. He is a global wealth strategist, successful entrepreneur, international speaker, astronaut, high adrenaline adventurer, and best-selling author. Nik Halik became a multimillionaire and amassed great wealth through savvy investments in property and the stock market in his late twenties. His group of companies has financially educated and life coached over 200,000 individuals globally. He is the real deal, creating millionaire clients across the globe. He is the author of *The Thrillionaire®*, intelligently orchestrated stories of adventure interspersed with financial wisdom and personal development advice. To order your copy now, go to www.TheThrillionaireLaunch.com.

Not only is Nik a successful entrepreneur, but he is also an avid, thrill-seeking adventurer. Among his various expeditions, he was one of the first explorers to dive down five miles and land on the bow of the Titanic. He has summited the highest mountains in the world and was one of the privileged select explorers to view the curvature of the earth from the edge of space. He is the very first flight-qualified and certified civilian astronaut from Australia and is also set to become the first ever Australian and private space explorer to rocket to outer space and live on Earth's only manned outpost in orbit, the International Space Station. He currently resides in Star City, Russia, at the prestigious Yuri Gagarin Cosmonaut Space Centre and among his private homes in the Greek Islands, Morocco, and Australia.

Winning When No One Believes in You but You

Gerald Walker

Winning in life is not an easy task, and it takes a lot of sacrifice, more than most people ever imagine. Winning for me meant making the sacrifice to put myself in a position to retire by the age of forty-five. I knew when I set that goal more than thirty years ago that it would be one hell of a task. Only about 1 percent of the 300 million Americans are in the position to accomplish that goal, and given that I come from a family where everyone retired on Social Security and no one had an inheritance, the odds were very much against me. But I always believed that if someone else could accomplish a goal, then I too had a shot at accomplishing that same goal.

The two books I have written, *Why African Americans Fear Doing Business in Nigeria* and *In and Out of the Game,* provide the full detail of how I was able to accomplish my goals. In this chapter, I will give you the short version.

When you set goals in life, you have to understand that to everyone else, your goals might seem impossible. But always remember that if you dream it, then hard work can help you achieve it. It will never be easy, and your family and friends will be the first ones to leave you. You have to want to win in order to be a winner—and have a fierce focus on your goal.

I always knew that I would never get paid what I was worth if I worked for someone else. But I was always successful when I worked for someone else, because no matter what job I performed, I always gave it 100 percent. I always tell the people who listen to me speak that if you have a written plan when you start your own business, and you work at least eight hours a day as you do on your job, it is almost impossible to fail. I can accept failing, but I can't accept not trying. The problem is that most people won't put forth that effort to even try.

I worked for a security company for four years, and seeing the company purchased for $14 million and sold for $103 million after that four-year period was disheartening because I was one of the main people contributing to the company making a $91 million profit in that time, yet I did not share in the profit. The experience taught me that you have to have your own business to reap that type of profit. Not only did I sell for the company, but I trained the sales force and made more than a six-figure income doing it. So after the sale of the company in 2001, I thought, if I'm going to make millions for someone again, then that person should be me. One of the other sales managers and I decided to start our own businesses at the same time, and here was the challenge. His father was rich; my wife and I had about fifty thousand dollars between both our savings and retirement. To get her retirement, my wife would have to quit her job of eight years. And this is what separates the winners from the losers: she quit her job and gave me her retirement money, and I cashed in my 401k and risked it all for my dream. The other manager started with $1 million, and I started with fifty thousand dollars. He started up without a business or marketing plan on paper, and I started with a written plan one or two months after he did. He started making two hundred thousand dollars per month in his first month, and I started making forty thousand per month. One year later, he was out of business, and my company was making two hundred thousand dollars per month.

The thing is, when I started, no one believed I could make it with such a small investment, but I had faith in two people—God and myself. It helped that I had a great business and marketing plan, but most of all what drove me was that I had no fear of failing. Most people thought I was crazy because I had an offer to make more than a six-figure income with the company that had purchased the company I'd worked for. If I would have listened to my family and friends, I would have taken that job, but I had faith in myself to win when no one believed in me but me.

My competition was multimillion- and multibillion-dollar security companies that offered to purchase my company, but when I wouldn't sell, they teamed up and tried to force me out of business, which almost worked. We had to go through an audit that almost put us out of business. It's hard to be on top of the business world, with one of the fastest-growing security companies, and three months later look up and all your employees are gone because one of your competitors offered a $2,500 bonus to each employee to leave. At that point, with the company in shambles, no one believed in me but me.

I think God allowed that adversity to happen because He knew I would have never reached my goals traveling the path I was on. I would have made a living but not a life. For average and ordinary people, a living is OK, but for extraordinary people, making a life for yourself means waking every day to do whatever you want to do. Changing the legacy of your family, so that poverty will never be an option, and having the funds to reach back and help other people is having a life, not just making a living.

If it had not been for the adversity I'd faced, I might not have looked at the opportunity in Nigeria, which was the opportunity that propelled me to reach my long-term goal.

The truth is, I was making OK money, but I was working about fourteen hours a day trying to manage a company with six offices in the state of Texas. A Nigerian guy who worked for me always talked to me about going to Nigeria to start a security business. I was one of those people who, if you loaded the boat and said we were going back to Africa, would not be on it. For most Americans, this journey would be way out of the box. He finally convinced me to do a feasibility study, and when it was completed, my eyes were opened to a whole new world. I still did not quite believe it until September 2004, when we went to Nigeria and I saw an incredible opportunity. But no one believed in it but me. This was a country that if you mention you are doing business there, most people would run from you. I will never forget the day I had dinner with two prominent professional athletes, a basketball player and a football player. I told them of the opportunity to start a business in Nigeria, and they laughed at me. Remembering that dinner was one thing that drove me whenever I thought about quitting.

I took on the challenge, and it proved to be one of the toughest challenges of my life. I learned that most people in life don't win because they don't want to suffer. I decided to suffer now while I have my health and strength, rather than when I am sixty-five or seventy years old and have to depend on Social Security to take care of my family and me because I didn't have the will to suffer and strive when I was younger. That is the ultimate form of suffering, and many of the baby boomers are headed that way. To me it is scarier than dying, and even if I don't accomplish my goals, at least I'll have given it everything I had. If that thought doesn't make you move and want to win, then I don't know what will.

Against all odds I started my security company in Nigeria with basically no investors and no help. I became the first African American to start a security company in Nigeria and the first African American to start an armored vehicle company and export a fleet of Level 6 armored cash-in-transit vehicles to Nigeria. There were billion-dollar companies that couldn't get their armored cash-in-transit products into that country because of fear. I had the courage to be the first to walk a path that had never been taken, and many times I sat in the hotel in Nigeria and cried because I didn't know how I would make the next day. Ten thousand miles away from home and not another American to talk to in sight. That was very tough; the only person I had to depend on was me. No one will ever be able to take away from me that I was the first to accomplish those two tasks in that country, and it will go down in history.

It took two years of hard work traveling to and from Nigeria to receive my first contract. Mostly everyone had abandoned me because they didn't believe it could be done. When you have a dream, sometimes your family and close friends can't see your vision.

Michael Jordan was a great player because he stayed and practiced after everyone else had gone, and he wasn't afraid to take the shot when the game was on the line. When your game is on the line, you can't let fear stop you from taking your shot. Most people might not know this, but Michael missed more game-winning shots than he made, but he never stopped shooting. To win, you have to keep shooting at your goal, because sooner or later you will hit the game-winning shot. All the disbelievers won't share your glory, but neither will they appreciate or know the suffering you went through to win—your story of success. That story is what you will have to go through and create in order to win. All winners have a successful story, so when God gets ready to click your light out for the last time, and you look back, what will be yours? Whatever you do, don't let fear steal your story.

About the Author

Gerald Walker was born to be a successful entrepreneur. After graduating from Grambling State University in 1984, he worked for Frito Lay and Southland Corporation for a combined seven years. He started his first company in 1992, which became one of the largest African American–owned travel agencies in Dallas, Texas. After relinquishing it in 1995, he started in the security industry and became the top sales person in Texas for four consecutive years.

In 2001 he started his own security company, which became the number one security company in the Dallas–Fort Worth area by the end of the first year in business, surpassing multimillion dollar companies in monthly security sales. In 2004, against all odds, he became the first African American to start a security company and implement the first solar power surveillance system for Shell Development Company in Nigeria. He partnered with a Nigerian friend and became the first American to start up a cash-in-transit company in Nigeria and was the first African American to deliver Level 6 armored cash-in-transit vehicles to Nigeria. He has never been afraid to go out of his comfort zone and take a risk, which has propelled him to build a multimillion-dollar international business. **For more information, contact Gerald Walker at 888-641-7582 Ext. 84; by email at** info@geraldwalker.net; or by mail: P.O. Box 4622, Cedar Hill, Texas 75106.

Dancing through a Dark, Dark Tunnel

Diana McKenzie

You know what? The great thing about a dark, dark tunnel is that there's usually a light at the end of it—at least for those with eyes to see and the willingness to keep walking. Let me tell you my story.

My Celtic mother had a rare and serious condition called systemic sclerosis, and she died when I was born. Doctors predicted that I'd die within a day, a week, a year—so the story goes—but stubbornly I kept on breathing. Inheriting her condition, I have had health challenges all my life, but I also inherited her gift as a healer, two sides of the same coin.

Adopted by a distant cousin, I grew up in the Kent countryside, a frail, bookish child who loved wandering alone in the woods. I developed a deep affinity with nature and a sense of spiritual presence, which has stayed with me all my life. At school I loved learning and couldn't imagine being anything other than a teacher. Not even becoming a dancer, gardener, or a veterinarian held more interest for me. Becoming a teacher was my mission, and in 1968 I was accepted at Goldsmith's College, University of London, regarded as the finest teacher-training college in England. I was going to study English literature. So far, so good.

Then came the hurly-burly of working in tough inner-city South London schools and youth projects, as a teacher, youth worker, counselor, trainer, and manager, projects where you either learn fast or run! I had thirty years of phenomenal experiences, including being thrown in the deep end with unfamiliar cultures and loving it, meeting fantastic young people brimming with creativity, fighting the system, hustling for resources, working with young people on the streets, fighting the system some more to save services, surviving occasional death threats, and then doing it all again the next day. Is that high stress or what!

In the 1980s Youth Service, most of us didn't know the meaning of work–life balance. We served the community 24/7, and eventually the strain took its toll as workers suffered heart attacks, strokes, and general ailments. Already registered as disabled, I collapsed with exhaustion in 1990. The spirit was willing, but the little legs gave way, and I was medically retired.

Does any of this sound familiar? Are you in control of your work, or does work control you? If you recognize the scenario, I seriously suggest you take a step back, a deep breath, and a long look. How's this for a cool epitaph: "Spent every waking hour at work."

With hindsight, I now see that alongside my positive self (caring, creative, courageous, passionate, with a burning sense of justice), I had a huge attitude problem. The dark side of passion, after all, is anger. I realized that a burning sense of justice is more often a burning sense of injustice. Ignorant of any wiser way, I was a volcano, a seething mass of rage and resentment, typical of the culture in that time and place. No wonder I was ill.

This is where it gets interesting. I've learned that it really is true that when one door closes, another will open. In debate with evangelists of another faith, I was resisting heavy pressure to leave my own path and join theirs. Suddenly, from the depths of my being, I made a vow. "Wherever the Spirit sends me, there will I go, willingly," I said. "Let the Spirit decide."

And that's a vow I have never broken. Quite magically, within twenty-four hours, I had met and joined a Japanese form of Buddhism and in the process made a leap that proved to be along a major learning curve. As a member of this lay Buddhist organization, I rapidly learned to chant, a very active and powerful form of meditation that I do to this day. This decision put my feet on the path of an amazing journey, discovering self and universal wisdoms. Through chanting, one raises one's own spiritual vibration, bringing increased wisdom, courage, compassion, and life force. That's the theory, and in my experience, it's true. I developed a strong, vibrant daily practice upon which all else is based.

Religious organizations, by their very nature, have teachings as well as practices, and I found myself swimming in a flow of ideas that were totally new to me—and swimming with no life belt! It was exciting and challenging, welcoming and disturbing, a sort of spiritual tumble-wash! I became a strong chanter and a seeking spirit. I learned voraciously from study, but more important, I was having *realizations* through my chanting, gaining incredible new insights into my own life and behavior, and into society in general. Seeds of wisdom were sprouting.

Just a few examples:

The Law of Cause and Effect—We create our karma. I began to see the patterns in events that affected me, and I saw they were not just random, disconnected events outside my control. At first, this felt embarrassing ("You mean, it's all *my* fault?!"), but then I grasped that if I made my karma with my causes (thoughts, words, and deeds), I could change my negative karma by changing my thoughts, words, and deeds. Wow, we really are in control. How liberating is that! (Obviously, you don't want to change the positive stuff: you deserve it; you made it. Enjoy!)

The Law of Attraction—What we attract in life is a reflection of what we give out. Again, we're in charge. If you don't like what you're getting, change the channel, raise your vibration! There are layers and complexities to grasp, but this is a great starting point for resolving disputes.

The Rule of Responsibility—It can be oh-so-tempting to blame. Blame is such a cozy comfort zone we can wear like old slippers. But blame stops us from questioning. Blame stops us growing.

The Attitude of Gratitude—Yes, folks, it's easy to be grateful for the good stuff, but apparently the bad stuff is really good stuff if you *get the lesson*. This concept is very simple in theory but difficult in practice. For years, I used to miss the pleasurable self-righteousness of a bloody good rant! The good news is, with a sincere daily practice, it gets easier. One day you realize you've got it, in blood and bone, and it's not theory anymore. It's *you*.

All the while at the core of my growth was and is the constant daily practice of chanting. Though my time in the Buddhist organization eventually ran its course, and I moved onward to follow my path, I cannot emphasize enough the importance of daily connection with the divine through the right form of meditation for you. There are many, and I encourage you to find yours.

One issue I never really explored through my chanting was my medical condition, which is essentially an allergy to my own antibodies, resulting in scleroderma, a connective tissue disease similar to lupus. Organ by organ, the condition had progressed, but I'd always coped. However, in 1997, under immense stress, I succumbed, with more and more organs affected, until in early 1998 I was diagnosed with systemic sclerosis, incurable and terminally at risk. Hospices were mentioned, and it seemed to be hand-in-your-dinner-plate time. And not only was I extremely sick, but my career was destroyed, and I was broke. Oooops!

What did I do? In a state of numbness, weak and coughing blood, I went to my altar and chanted, knowing the time had come to prove my faith—coughing and chanting, coughing and chanting. Eventually, a volcanic rebellion began to rise within, and I found myself saying, "No! I'm not having it. I've still got work to do!" I vowed with my whole being to halt, turn, and cure my physical condition. Again, I hurled the golden javelin of Intention and felt at peace, that all was well. Surprisingly, I realized that death will come as an old friend when it's my time. But not yet.

A word about intention. Napoleon Hill wrote a classic, *Think and Grow Rich*. Well, we can use that idea. It's "Think and Grow Anything," so why not "Think and Grow Healthy." Use your intention and fill in the blanks.

The next year was undeniably a very dark time but also a huge learning experience. I used my faith, knowledge, and connection with Source to *battle* my illness, and through chanting, I uncovered the deep-rooted karma that resulted in such a debilitating condition. Now that was an insight, and then some! Against the odds, slowly, I began to recover.

As I traveled this journey, fascinating things began to happen. As if by magic, the right doctors, books, tapes, complementary therapies, and people I needed all flowed into my life like ripe plums dropping from a tree. Synchronicity! In rhythm with the universe! This was becoming seriously cool.

I was reading, learning, and *applying* so many new ideas that were from the personal development world. What is more, as I chanted, I was having visions of a golden fountain flowing through me. I decided to play with this golden light, visualizing my blood circulating as pure gold and bathing my damaged lungs. It really worked, and I felt empowered. I recommend it. Visualize away, folks. You've got the power, too.

And guess what? As I began to heal, I was getting interested in the process. I was enjoying myself, and the battle became a dance—a totally different, far more healing energy. This was the light at the end of the tunnel. I embraced the dark time as the gateway to a bright life of purpose. I knew that I wanted to share with others what I was fortunate enough to be learning, and then I was struck by a question: "Why isn't this taught in schools?"

When still very frail, I vowed that one day I would teach what I wanted, to whom I wanted, on my terms, sharing ancient and modern wisdoms, two sides of the same coin. I would help put other people's feet on the first steps of the spiritual journey, let them walk it how they choose. Thus was born my business, Bright Lives, and also The Kaizen Initiative, a Social Enterprise Project to work in schools and the community. It's taken a while, but I'm doing it.

Bright Lives' flagship workshop is "Find the Pearl Within: First Steps to Awaken Your Spiritual Self," valuable for anyone but designed for people who are ready to explore their spirituality but are unsure where to start. Supporting you to start, sure footed and free, is my purpose and my pleasure. Come, join me.

My definition of spirituality? Imagine yourself as a tree, the branches of your life spreading out—family, work, health, finances, leisure, politics, and so forth. The roots of your tree grow deep into the rich, fertile soil of spirit. As the roots nourish all branches with fertility, so our connection with divine spirit through developed, daily practice nourishes all aspects of our lives. We become in rhythm, harmony, and balance with the universe, and in love with life. To me, that is true spirituality. What's your definition?

Cooperating with the Youth Office, I've returned as a volunteer to work with youth in my area, Peckham, South London (arguably the nearest thing Britain has to the hood), delivering personal development seminars to groups in youth clubs. It's all happening here and could be in your area, too. Got any ideas, skills, visions, contacts to offer? Yes? Then go for it!

Last, I have huge strategies to take this learning nationwide in our schools. It will happen. Bothered by the pressure of trying to achieve my whole vision before retirement, imminent in 2008, I came to a decision. Don't retire, just keep on keeping on. That solves that problem. Sixty is the new forty, and we, ladies and gentlemen of a certain age, are marvelous. We can do it! There is a rising wave of awakening, young and old, and we are all droplets in The Wave. Let's move it and shake it together.

Why am I sharing this with you? Well, without my highly developed spiritual practice, I could not possibly have turned this illness. I would have lacked the tools and necessary understanding. I would have died. But there's nothing I've done that you can't do too, if you only choose to develop yourself. Make it your intention to grow *now*. Don't wait until you're on the Titanic before you learn to swim.

Is this it? Am I done? Not at all. When dreams are achieved, it's time to start dreaming bigger dreams that become plans, then strategies, then achievements. And you know what? It's such *fun!*

What are your dreams? Make them *big!*

My dreams have always been global, for a peaceful, prosperous, Earth-loving world. Twenty-five years ago, I vowed my life in service to the Spirit, and I know in blood and bone exactly where I'm headed, and it's a brilliant, hard, challenging, dangerous, wonderful road—but that's for another book.

Blessed be.

About the Author

A Celt from the Scottish Highlands, Diana McKenzie grew up in the orchards, woods, and fields of the Kent countryside in England. She then spent more than three decades in tough inner-city London as a teacher, youth worker, counselor, and trainer. In 2005, Diana made a quantum leap forward and set up her own business, Bright Lives, based in London and offering a range of personal development workshops and coaching for individuals, groups, and teams. She is a qualified teacher, youth worker, trainer, coach, counselor, consultant, public speaker, and author, and she specializes in spiritual development. Her flagship workshop is "Find the Pearl Within—First Steps to Awaken Your Spiritual Self." Furthermore, combining her knowledge, life experience, and counseling and coaching skills, plus her inherited abilities as a healer, Diana offers her own unique process—life healing.

Increasingly, in demand as a public speaker and as a panelist on radio and television, Diana is a member of the globally empowering Success University and is eagerly spreading the benefits to her community. For more information about Diana, see her website, www.brightlives.co.uk, or email her at info@brightlives.co.uk. For more information about Success University, see www.brightlives.successuniversity.com.

Everybody Needs a Hero

Soojay Devraj

When I was eight years old, my father decided to follow his dreams and build a mansion in another country. He took me with him, leaving the rest of my brothers and my sister behind with my grandparents. I was always an adventurous child, wanting to explore and try new things. Leaving the comfort and safety of my grandparents' home to go to a new land was one big adventure, especially exciting because I did not know what to expect.

Little did I know how isolated I would feel because my parents were both working, and I had nobody to play with. I turned to eating for comfort and to ease my loneliness, and I dived into adventure novels, where danger lurks behind every bend, to pass the time until my parents arrived home. My parents owned a supermarket, where they worked long hours. My mother took the easy route when preparing lunch for me. Instead of making me a healthy lunch, she gave me fast food from the supermarket: pies, milkshakes, chocolates, cakes, biscuits, burgers, chips. This worsened my isolation.

Besides developing a sweet tooth, I also developed into a really fat kid. I was so fat that people started calling me thunder thighs, fatso, chubby, and tubby. This was my first experience with labeling, one of the most crushing and psychologically damaging things anybody can do to children because of the long-term effects it has on their confidence and self-esteem. It amazes me that people are quick to say something bad about another person but find it hard to say anything good about that person. The same effort and energy these people used to put me down could have been used to lift me up.

We are programmed right through school to compete against each other by putting each other down so that we can go to the top. What we should have been taught was to create, not to compete against each other (other than in sports, where there generally is only one winner). We could have chosen the creative route, where there is an abundance of material to use in winning and where you can help the next person win also, because when another person wins using the creative route, it does not take anything away from you.

All substance in a creative environment is unlimited—there is more than enough for everybody. Taking the creative path generally requires the assistance of other people to succeed, and with more than 6 billion people on our planet, there is no shortage of potential creative assistance. If we had been taught in school to work *with* each other instead of against each other, we would all be a lot happier and more productive.

Strangely enough, the only time I found this happening was when I was working on my MBA. We had to work in teams from the beginning to the end of our studies. This strategy proved very successful because the weakness of the individual was balanced by the strengths of the other team members. Now imagine if we were taught this from the time we entered our educational system. If we'd used a teamwork strategy, we all would have graduated from high school as winners—instead of whiners, wondering what to do next.

No wonder so many recent graduates are messed up. After twelve years of programming that taught them to work as individuals, they suddenly enter the workplace where everybody works as a team, something they were never taught to do. This causes major stress. They don't know how to tell their boss that they don't know how to work in a team and quietly suffer in silence hoping that nobody will notice their incompetence. So instead of being brave enough to tell the truth, they suffer verbal abuse by their colleagues or boss for being incompetent while they are learning teamwork skills on the job. It would have been so easy to teach them in school. No wonder there are so many dysfunctional employees and entrepreneurs; they were never taught the basics of working as a team.

After getting so fat as a child, with people constantly pointing fingers at me and ridiculing me, I resorted to becoming a recluse, hidden away in my room, eating even more junk food and drowning my sorrows in fizzy drinks. When I was ten years old, my younger sister moved from my grandparents' home to live with us. I was very happy to have company, but my younger sister won every academic award and sports trophy the school had. This made it even worse for me. I was now the ugly duckling who could not match the achievements of his younger sister. There had to be something wrong with me. How could I argue? The evidence was there in the form of my sister. She was a performer. I was a non-performer. This crushed me even further.

When I was thirteen years old, my two older brothers moved in with us from my grandparents' home. We were finally all together in high school. The ridiculing carried on. I was often called to the front of the class by my tenth-grade math teacher and told to explain, for example, how I got four out of twenty-five on an algebra test. The usual laughing and finger pointing ensued. My math teacher then told me my fortune, how I was stupid and destined to be a bum, standing on the street corners, begging for money.

One day my eldest brother, Venu, who was the school jock, called me into his room and asked me a question that would change my life. He asked me whether I wanted to keep allowing people to laugh and make fun of me or do something about it. What a question! The moment of truth had arrived. I knew that whatever answer I gave, it would change my life forever. This was a self-fulfilling prophecy. Now, what was so different this time? I had wanted the ridiculing to stop in the past, but it never did. It was different this time because I was taking responsibility, making the decision to change and confessing it over my life. Remember, words have power, and whatever I was about to say would become true in my life because I said it.

I remember feeling very weak and hot, as though I had a fever, with my mouth going dry. I murmured, "I want to do something about it." Venu then asked me how badly I wanted it. I said, "Really badly."

He said, "Are you prepared to do whatever it takes to make the change even if you don't like the changes?"

I said, "Yes." I mean, who was I to doubt Venu? He was the school hero, the most outstanding athlete, feared by his enemies because of his muscles, adored by the girls in the school because of his popularity, a charismatic person who exuded charm and drew people to him. The whole school idolized him, including me. I often escaped getting a beating by thugs just because I told them that I was Venu's brother. I was safe under his protective shadow when I was in school.

I wanted more than anything in the world to be just like him, He was my hero. So when he asked all those questions, I naturally said "yes," hoping that he would give me some magical formula or potion that would instantly make me just like him. Little did I realize what I had committed to. It was the beginning of discipline, which would shape me into a hero, too.

I did not know, in essence, what the discussion in Venu's room was all about. It was actually a contract between a mentor (Venu) and a student (me). Trust me when I tell you that finding someone who has achieved the results you are looking for and is willing to coach you is invaluable. This is how my first mentor, Venu, changed my life.

It started with jogging every day. In the beginning, it was really painful and embarrassing. When I could not run uphill because I was so fat, he kicked me from the back, which was mortifying, especially when people were around. This motivated me to run so I wouldn't get kicked in the butt. I used to cry because it was so painful and humiliating. My chest wheezed, and I could hardly breathe. As each day passed, though, I got stronger and stronger. I did pressups with Venu on my back. My physique, stamina, and fitness level changed. I could hardly recognize myself after three months. My self-esteem and confidence improved. I became a super athlete, eventually winning the national championship in surf lifesaving.

With the encouragement of Venu, I set a goal of earning a master's degree in business administration in my quest for financial freedom. Many people said that I should not attempt it and predicted I would fail because I was too young and inexperienced. They went out of their way to discourage me. This was one of the biggest hurdles in my life, but I overcame it. Many people with higher IQs than I have quit the program when they crumbled under the pressure. I guess they never got kicked in the butt before for falling behind. Venu taught me that no matter who you are, as long as you desire something badly enough and are willing to take the action that leads you to your goal and never give up until you get there, anything is possible!

Success is nothing more than a few simple disciplines,
practiced every day.
—Jim Rohn

The Light Switch

Being unsuccessful and failing is like groping around for the light switch in a dark room. You constantly stumble and even fall. Others in the room who also failed to find the light switch, or perhaps prefer the dark, keep telling you that you won't succeed. But the minute you find the switch and the light comes on, the darkness disappears. All the voices of discouragement disappear. And you thank God you never listened to any of them. You stuck to your guns and carried on until you found your light switch. Now, this light switch could be the business, job, partner, house, car, husband or wife that everyone else believes is wrong for you but that you know deep down in your gut is right.

Let Go

By the time I completed my MBA degree, I never came across any of the people who had put me down in the past. Nor are these people part of my future. This is one of the *key lessons* you must learn if you want to be successful. *You have to let go of all the people who no longer serve your interests.* They have served the purpose for which they have been placed in your company, and you can hope you added value to their lives as well. It is time for you to move on. As Johnny Wimbrey puts it, "Don't be a parked car." We all know what dogs do to parked cars. So if you don't want these family members or friends to crush your dreams, if they are no longer helping you succeed or develop, then it is time to part company with them and get new friends who will help you achieve the next level of personal development and success. This is a continuous cycle and never comes to an end until you no longer want to succeed or develop any further.

For those who need stability in their lives, the good news is that, although you will be constantly gaining new friends and associates, you will still have the same spouse and kids. God seems to have a way of sorting out people. Like attracts like. I guess that is why the rich stay with the rich and the poor stay with the poor. I used to imagine bumping into my tenth-grade math teacher and telling him that I am far more educated than he his, but I know this will never happen because I have found my light switch—success. The minute I hit the light switch, all the dark forces in my life disappeared, never to be seen again.

Words Have Power to Create Your Future

The Bible says that "death and life are in the power of the tongue" (Proverbs 18:21, NKJV). God says choose life by speaking words that give life. Whatever you are constantly speaking about, to yourself or other people, is what eventually happens to you. This is the law of sowing and reaping. There is no escape from this spiritual law. Whatever you sow, you will reap. This is how, as Brian Tracy put it, "you are the architect of your own destiny." You design your life by the words you speak. Wise men and women are careful about what they confess over their lives with the words they speak. *Always make sure your words are positive.* A lot of people speak words of negativity and destruction, which eventually manifests in their life because they have called it upon themselves by always speaking negative words. *Words have power!*

> *So shall My word be that goes forth from My mouth. It shall not return to me void, but it shall accomplish what I please, and it shall prosper in the thing for which I sent it.*
> —Isaiah 55:11

Muhammad Ali applied this knowledge to becoming the greatest heavyweight boxer in the world. He was an unknown boxer who kept telling himself, "I am the greatest." This eventually sunk into his subconscious. His physical condition, stamina, and boxing skills all changed to manifest what he said all the time. He said it so often and so loudly that even his opponents believed him. He had often won the fight before even stepping into the ring because he had already beaten his opponents psychologically. The ring was just a formality to manifest what he already believed would happen.

Four-Step Action Plan to Get What You Want

Another reason to be careful about the words you speak is that they bring the unseen into the seen, as it is written, "Therefore I say to you, whatever things you ask when you pray, believe that you receive them, and you will have them" (Mark 11:24). This is the power of your belief and faith in yourself and in God that we all have been born and blessed with, but only a few apply it. It is this internal power that we all have within us that converts our thoughts into realities. To access this power, all you have to do is

1. *focus* on what you want;
2. *think* night and day about what you want;
3. *visualize* for fifteen minutes a day, in a quiet room with your eyes closed, how it will feel when you have it; and
4. *give thanks to God* for giving it to you—it will come faster to you if you do!

Become a Master at Asking

Asking is the beginning of receiving. Make sure you don't go to the ocean with a teaspoon. At least take a bucket so the kids won't laugh at you.

—Jim Rohn

Ask and you shall receive! We are all divinely connected, and *only by asking God for help* with something you want to accomplish can God make arrangements for you to receive the help from the right people who suddenly come into your life. As it is written, "So I say to you, ask, and it will be given to you; seek, and you will find; knock, and it will be opened to you. For everyone who asks, receives, and he who seeks finds, and to him who knocks it will be opened" (Luke 11:9-10).

Give thanks for all that you have and you will be blessed with more of it.

Being in a constant state of gratitude to your creator allows more good things to flow your way.

About the Author

Soojay Devraj has a master's degree in business administration from the University of Wales. He has proved that even educated people can become financially free. He reached the top of Success University, a network marketing company specializing in personal development, in only fourteen months, not fourteen years. He is currently spreading the word of Success Education as the first ambassador for Success University in Africa. Soojay finally achieved his dream of financial freedom through network marketing after trying the traditional route to getting rich from clothing manufacturing, video store franchising, and working at top corporate jobs. The full story of Soojay Devraj's extraordinary climb to the top will be revealed in his book *From Zero to Hero* (to be released).

To get started with the Success University and receive a free e-book, *Think and Grow Rich,* by Napoleon Hill, visit http://www.cashking. biz. You can contact Soojay Devraj at 27 11 482 9743 (telephone); 27 82 577 8469 (mobile); or by email: soojaysu@yahoo.com.

Back to Front

Rebecca Lennox

Most of us, if we think about it, have much to be happy and grateful about. We are generally healthy, with all our basic needs met and much more. On paper, life should be just perfect, yet so many people feel like they're stuck on a treadmill, going nowhere fast. They believe the grass is always greener on the other side and are constantly searching for something more, somebody better, or some true fulfillment in their lives.

It's like being a yacht in the harbor, where it's safe. We may long to be out on the high seas, but often we are afraid of setting sail in a new, or any particular, direction because we're uncertain of our final destination and outcome. And yet the adventure, excitement, and rewards can be achieved only after we've set sail and are out on the big, unknown ocean. Sure, there will be obstacles to overcome along the way. We'll have to tack on occasion to adjust to the outside elements and to fine-tune our direction, but once we've set our general course, why don't we just enjoy the journey?

Many people don't want to take responsibility or be accountable for their actions. We live in a blame culture, and it's easy to explain away failures by blaming someone or something outside our control. I believe a fear of failure or rejection holds many of us back from making a change, because making a change means breaking habits we have developed over a lifetime—not to mention the pressure from friends and family who feel most comfortable seeing us behave in the way we always have. Many people would rather remain miserable than make the effort to step outside their comfort zone. It's incredible just how many people hate their jobs and yet dread being fired.

What was quite shocking and surprising to me was that I was running on this very treadmill and not sure how to get off, even though I'd always considered myself a proactive, driven, motivated, positive, and generally happy person. I felt trapped, not feeling good about my situation or how I was viewing myself. I was the yacht still tied up in the harbor, with the ability to set my beautiful sails and maximize my potential, but that just was not going to happen if I stayed in port.

When your "why" is strong enough, it doesn't matter that you don't know "how" you're going to achieve your goal before you take that first step!

My overall desire to discover my life purpose, and the immediate desire I had to achieve a couple of big goals enabled me to decide to change the way I was running my life. Taking the first step was the most difficult, but after that, the solutions kept presenting themselves to me just at the point I was ready. As a result, I have transformed my life and have loved every minute of the journey. I've never looked back since the moment I made the decision, so if you're reading this knowing that you're on that treadmill, don't wait any longer—you can step off it right now. Remember, "Nothing changes if nothing changes!"

Simply by following a few simple rules for success like I did, you can make any change toward greater fulfillment and ultimate happiness in your life:

1. Develop your life purpose; make sure that it is bigger than you are.

2. Have a strong and definite desire to reach a goal, one that should both excite and scare you.

3. Visualize achieving your goal, and make sure the image is so vivid in your mind that you believe you've already achieved it.

4. Take time to formulate a definite plan for carrying out your desire and begin at once, even if you don't feel completely ready.

5. Focus on taking steps you *know* you can take *right now* that will move you in the direction of your desires. There will be some steps in your plan that you don't know *how* to achieve, but this does not matter; the answer will present itself to you at the perfect moment.

Les Brown once said something that has stuck with me ever since I heard it, and I think it's sound advice for anyone worried about taking that first step toward a new and improved life: "You don't have to be great to get started, but you have to get started to be great!" If you want your life to be different, you simply have to take that first step.

I'm now going to share with you a few pivotal moments in my life and the resulting transformations that have led me toward becoming a better, happier, and more fulfilled person. In so doing, I hope that my experiences and insights will both resonate with you and inspire you to find your better self.

The Successful High-Flying Business Woman

Up until I was approaching the big 3-0, the word "success" to me meant being a powerful, well-respected businesswoman with a great presence, holding down and excelling in various management roles, and working my way up the career ladder. I confess to having enjoyed many aspects of this high-powered, stressful, and fast-moving lifestyle, traveling across the globe, frequenting some of the top prestigious hotels and restaurants, and living a couple of years in the beautiful city of Paris.

It appeared to me that most women holding senior positions in the business world, and certainly in the pharmaceutical industry I was so accustomed to, were single, meaning no husbands or children to look after. I also noticed that they tended to have a tough exterior and rarely showed any emotion. Frankly, I found many of these women to be manipulative, selfish, and verging on ruthless. These qualities seemed to be prerequisites for female executives, who constantly needed to prove themselves in a male-dominated world. I aspired to be like them and modeled this kind of woman, working hard to display some of these characteristics.

> *"Success" can mean so much more than reaching the pinnacle*
> *of the career ladder.*

I didn't notice it for many years, but I eventually discovered that an internal conflict had always gone on inside me. Something felt out of synchronicity with what I was all about and my inner being, but I just hadn't realized it. I was headstrong and determined to keep pushing onward and upward until finally it dawned on me that many of the career decisions I was making were a result of what I thought would be expected of me—by whom, I will never know. I came to realize that I was the one pressuring myself. I believed that to be successful in life, I had to succeed in a career by getting all the way to the top and becoming the CEO. What was all that about? Can't success mean so much more?

> *Are you really a human being and not just a human doing and achieving?*

At every point in my life I have achieved, achieved, and achieved, in academics, in business, in athletics—I won many sporting accolades in tennis, hockey, swimming, and running. Most of my friends, family, and boyfriends could never keep up with me. I worked very hard, socialized even harder, and exercised like mad. Whenever I had holiday, I was always off to the most remote part of the world with a backpack on, trekking up to the summit of a huge peak or venturing into some danger zone on my own, causing my parents constant worry.

I have never understood what I was trying to prove, but I always felt it necessary to overcome another challenge. I'd been brought up with a "live life to the fullest" and "work hard play hard" attitude, and yet I was beginning to wonder how long I would be able to continue this lifestyle or have the desire to keep up the pace. Problem was, I didn't know any different.

Peeling off the Layers

I began questioning whether I truly felt fulfilled in my career and, more important, in my life as a whole. I was actually living life "back to front." I had the successful career in the bag, and yet now I wanted to get back to the real me. Looking inward for the first time, I became aware of some of my behavioral patterns. Some things consistently showed up that were really not helpful to me, but they were clearly running through all aspects of my life. Here are just a few examples:

- I was obsessed with being very popular among all my friends and colleagues and hated any form of conflict.
- I wanted to please others all the time and rarely made any time for me. I aspired to be everything to everybody—an impossible task, and deep inside, I felt like I was nothing to anyone.
- I aspired to be perfect, or appear perfect to others, and to follow the model career path, which no one can follow to perfection.
- I was highly competitive with others and mostly with myself, setting ridiculously high expectations and often beating myself up for failing to meet them.
- I was exceptionally strong and independent, rarely asking for help or, God forbid, showing signs of emotion like shedding a tear, because those are signs of "weakness."
- I did not have the courage to say "no," for fear of letting anybody down or being rejected.

Whether I consciously recognized it or not, trying to keep up this appearance every single day was completely tiring and wearing.

Asking for help is a sign of strength, not weakness.

I was strongly encouraged by a colleague and close friend to participate in an intense and intimate personal development course that had helped him transform his own life. He could sense I would benefit hugely from having some guidance and support in getting some clarity. For the first time in my life, I was open to asking for help to enable me to see things as they truly were and to see myself as I truly was. Simply by attending the course, I too had a massive personal breakthrough.

The uniqueness of this course was its exceptionally personal and intimate style, amazing support group, and the safe environment it provided, where nobody was judging me. There was no possibility to hide, but only to step up and open up. Having been labeled the control freak within the group by the master practitioner and facilitator of the course, I was challenged to let go and give myself a break. By making this my focus during the course, I had two big realizations:

1. Live in the moment. I had always believed I was living life to the fullest, and yet now I realized my big internal conflict was that deep down, I didn't believe I was really living at all. I saw my life as either in front of me or behind me and not really in the here and now. This was such a huge wake-up call for me. I now realized there was little point in wasting energy regretting what did or did not happen in the past or worrying what may or may not happen in the future. From that day forward, I began to understand the power in *now!* The "here and now" is the only place and time we can be in, so it was a truly wonderful and liberating feeling to let go and to just enjoy being in the present.

2. Accept and love myself. The profound experience during this course got to my core essence through a deep and emotionally painful process. I had spent so many years wanting to be perfect, trying to please other people, needing to be liked, and worrying what others thought of me. For the first time I really let go and for once was totally honest with myself. I was learning to accept the real me, warts and all. Only when I began to truly accept and *love* me for who I really was could I truly give, please, or love anybody else.

What do you really want and what will make you happy?

The breakthrough moment within my career finally happened a couple of years ago. I had found the answer, or rather, the pivotal question: Why was I struggling to climb up to the next rung of the ladder in my career when the ladder was leaning against the wrong wall for me? *Crazy!*

The personal development I had focused on over the previous few years had helped me begin to find my essence and get back to the core of who I really am. The next big question was to figure out what I really wanted in and for my life. Answering the three questions below was the final trigger for me to have the courage to break from my twelve-year career within the pharmaceutical industry:

- What would you do if you had all the money in the world?
- What would you do if you had six months to live?
- What would you do if you knew you absolutely could not fail?

Life is not a dress rehearsal, and I have so much I want to accomplish. I was ready to start living and fulfilling a potential within me. I had finally begun to listen to my inner self, and I felt contentment and confidence that I was doing the right thing by letting go of the safety of being employed by a huge company. The free-spirited Becky was ready to shine through and push the corporate businesswoman Rebecca back into her box. I was ready to follow my heart and push through new boundaries on a more fulfilling path in my life journey. The bud within me had been closed for so many years, but now it was about to burst into blossom.

Finding a Bigger Purpose

It is so important to feel like I am making a difference and adding value to a greater cause. Following my resignation from my global marketing role in Paris, I felt instantly compelled to give my time and energy to a charity. The most important thing was to feel like I could make a difference, however small, and to help others less fortunate or experienced than myself. I set off to be a project leader for Raleigh International, working with young adult volunteers in remote areas of the developing world to carry out specific projects in the community and environment. What an amazing adventure. It allowed the real me to shine through, and I felt I was making a difference and adding some value not only to the remote and exceptionally poor community in Nicaragua where I worked, which now had a school, but also to the young volunteers whom I guided and mentored. Finally, I felt free from the corporate world telling me what I must or must not do.

Listen to your inner voice, have faith, and trust you are on the right path. The answer will come to you at the right moment.

I knew I was on a different path now but had no real idea which one. I had left behind the security and all that comes with being part of a big organization, and I was now both scared and excited about the endless choices out there for me to pursue. Now that my mind and heart were open to all these opportunities, I knew I could never go back. I also knew that whichever path I chose would be the right one for me.

An experienced traveler friend said to me many years ago that once you start traveling, you will get the travel bug, and it never goes away. How true that is. He said this to me when we were traveling together on an overland truck through Africa when I was twenty-one, and I have not stopped traveling since.

After returning from my charity work in Central America, I realized the experience had only cemented my desire to explore more of the world. I did not want to explore merely as a backpacker, however. I wanted to contribute toward a greater cause, especially in areas of the developing world where there is a need for help and support. This is definitely the direction of the path leading toward my bigger life purpose, so much so that I have a shiver down my spine when I visualize creating and leading a very worthwhile, large-scale project in a country of need. I have the why, and I know the how will come to me at the right moment.

Before going off to "save the world," however, I felt it was important for me to pursue a spiritual journey to deepen my knowledge, understanding, and practice of yoga. As a qualified teacher and practicing yogi, I was completely taken in by my previous visit to India, where I had done a month-long retreat in an Ashram in Kerala. The plan for this year was to spend some time really exploring the country, looking for opportunities to give my time to help others, and to make a spiritual journey of self-discovery.

Getting Back in Front

Learn from the key lesson that comes with each setback in life.

Life doesn't always go according to plan, and a month after returning to England after my charity work, I was knocked for six with a back injury. Now, eighteen months after being struck by the first severe pains, I realize that this setback had been creeping up on me, subconsciously, over a couple of years. It wasn't even a serious back injury, but it was serious enough to prevent me from being the supreme active and sporty person, doing all the things I was convinced I so loved in my life.

This was the hardest obstacle I have had to overcome, and I spent many hours distraught at the prospect of never being able to walk pain-free again, let alone being able to get back on a tennis court, practice yoga, run, or continue my salsa dancing. It took several weeks for it to sink in that I was going to be physically inactive for some time. Getting out of bed in the morning was now an effort. I felt totally helpless and completely reliant on others to help me…the support from my family was truly amazing and feel so fortunate and privileged to have them around me and love them more than words can say.

I had to put my plans for traveling to India on hold. For the first time in my life, I was not physically able to run away to the other side of the world, which was what I had always been used to doing. Initially I felt trapped and dependent, and that something good would come out of this situation was not a possibility in my mind.

Listen to your body, and at times, slow down and let go!

It was payback time. I had abused my body physically and mentally for many years with excessive sports activities and a stressful career, both of which must have had an enormous impact on my back. The physical symptoms alone were excruciating and debilitating, but there was much more involved; there was a strong link between where I was mentally and emotionally. The life transition I was going through was manifesting itself through my back pain, and to heal my back, I would need to just stop and give myself time to take stock of where I was in my life and what was really important to me. I was in a period of shift from having spent many years being a headstrong, successful corporate businesswoman to *letting go* of that, listening to my inner voice, and following my heart to become the person I truly am. This was the only way to get myself back in front.

Loving the Life I Live and Living the Life I Love!

As disappointed as I was initially when my back sidelined me from all my activities, to my surprise, I also felt a sense of mental and emotional relief. I felt free. I made the decision to totally accept my situation and continue to be super positive. This allowed me to put my energies into some new activities and different kinds of people than I was familiar with in my sporty world.

I kept on track with a very tight recovery program that included keeping myself in a positive mental attitude as well as getting the best physical treatment. Reciting my daily affirmation—*"Every day in every way my back is getting better and better!"*—regularly doing an emotional freedom technique, and meditating all helped me overcome the physical pain as well as keeping me relaxed and in the best positive state. By seizing the moment and embracing these changes, I found that some great new opportunities opened up for me. By believing in myself and projecting forward strongly— seeing myself being fit and healthy once again—by following *The*

Secret principle of the law of attraction, the idea that like attracts like, special gifts have been coming to me.

The most amazing thing I want to share is that I attracted somebody very special into my life. This person had become a great friend and colleague during the time I worked for the charity in Nicaragua, and our relationship grew even stronger on our return to the UK. For the first time in my life, I felt ready to commit 100 percent to a relationship and not have one toe dipped outside. He is completely gorgeous in every sense of the word, one of the most kind and generous people I have ever met, and somehow he just makes me want to be a better person. We are very similar and yet so different, but at heart we are both fun-loving people. I really feel like I am a teenager again when we are together. Most important, we totally trust each other, and we have a deep unspoken connection.

Love unconditionally, however risky it may feel!

I am a strong individual and have always been *independent,* and yet I am striving for *interdependence,* where together as a couple and team, we will be even stronger and more awesome than we are as two individuals. This is when I am most happy.

There is no certainty of what the future holds for our relationship, of course. But in a switch from my previous behavior of holding back slightly in relationships, I am loving him with all my heart. I may get hurt, but the joy and happiness of being intimate with somebody special far outweighs this slight fear of feeling vulnerable. You see, I have fully embraced the old adage "it is better to have loved and lost than never to have loved at all."

Think and Grow Rich and *Think Big, Win Big*

The possibilities are infinite. My boyfriend and I participated in several workshops and seminars focusing on creating wealth and becoming millionaires through the mindset of multiple streams of income. These special events, led by true inspirational masters in their field, along with being included in a Mastermind group studying the Napoleon Hill bestseller *Think and Grow Rich*, have transformed the way we think. We're now thinking big with the idea of winning big. We both have more confidence to pursue a big idea, focus on the goal, make a decision, take that first action step, and persist until we get the desired result. Only weeks after completing the course, we are now about to launch an extremely exciting Internet business that is still secret—but watch this space!

My Mastermind group also helped me decide to expand the property business I started with my brother a few years ago. Subsequently, we have grown our portfolio in the student-buy-to-let market and continue to develop our current properties. My increased confidence and decision-making ability has also enabled me to seize an opportunity to invest abroad, which is incredibly exciting.

Complete Career Shift

One of the most impulsive decisions I made about six months ago, just at the time my back was feeling stronger, was to retrain to become a personal trainer and sports massage therapist. This has been at the back of my mind for many years. I'd trained myself toward an elite level of peak performance in several sports, and over the years, I suffered many sports-related injuries. Another factor in my decision, after occasionally wondering why I never pursued my early dreams of going into medicine, was a strong desire to make a difference in people's health and well-being.

I was recently awarded my diploma qualification, having absolutely loved the intensive learning and studying the course required. Now is a very exciting and scary time for me, starting at the beginning to build up my own business from scratch, but this time it is on my terms and I am the boss. I know I just have to go for it and that I will fall flat on my face a few times. But I also know I'll bounce back and learn from the experience and continue to grow and improve. One of my all-time favorite quotes sums up my philosophy about the inevitable pitfalls on the way to success: "There is no such thing as failure—just a good learn." I am not one to give up easily, so rest assured I will continue to "keep on keeping on."

Things Happen for a Reason

I believe that things really do happen for a reason. I learned and benefited so much during what I'd initially thought would be a nightmare time in my life. I am so happy and grateful that I was burdened with this back injury because many of these exciting opportunities wouldn't have come to me if everything had gone according to my original plan of traveling around trying to find myself in India. The injury and all that flowed from it was meant to be.

One of the biggest lessons I learned while deciding to leave the corporate world (which to many of you will seem obvious but took me so long to understand) is that being successful doesn't have to mean achieving great heights in a given career at the cost of everything else. This could result in missing so much of what life has to offer. Other things in my life every day are becoming much more important to me, like being a successful daughter, friend, partner, wife, and, who knows, possibly even a successful mother one day.

I have no idea what the future holds for me, and that is just perfect. I'm enjoying living in the moment and having fun exploring opportunities and breaking outside my comfort zone to try new things and grow in the process of having lots of "good learns." I am in a beautiful place of uncertainty right now and am wearing my T-shirt with "Just for today" on one side and "Don't worry, be happy!" on the other. I'm loving living in the moment.

I've got some big ideas and goals for the future and am becoming clearer each day on my life purpose. Importantly, though, I'm going to continue to love each step of the journey and not feel attached to the outcome. I'll keep on trusting and following my heart, being true to myself, and I will continue to unconditionally love and give to all people without wanting anything in return. I realize I've done things in my life in a "back to front" kind of way. Now I'm happy to be back to being the real me and on the right path, where my journey of self-discovery will continue and the bud inside will start to blossom into a beautiful flower.

I certainly intend to "live full and die empty," and not the other way around. I urge you to do the same.

About the Author

After graduating from Cambridge University in England with a BA honors in natural sciences and the highest British university sporting accolade—two Blues for hockey and running—Rebecca started her career within sales and marketing in the pharmaceutical industry with the U.S. company Merck based in London. She worked in various roles within Merck before moving to Novartis and then a high-profile role within the global marketing team of Sanofi-aventis, where she spent a couple of years based in their headquarters in Paris.

Rebecca is a Neuro-Linguistic Programming (NLP) practitioner and recently qualified as a personal trainer, sports massage therapist, and yoga teacher. She is excited about working with many different kinds of people to help them reach their goals around health, fitness, and general well-being. For more information on Becky, please visit www.rebeccalennox.com or contact her at 44 (0) 773 622 6950 or via email at becky@rebeccalennox.com.

Stepping Out to Work with a Purpose

Dion Johnson

Everyone had already gone home; I sat at my desk and glanced at the clock.... 7pm. I switched off my computer for the last time with one great sigh of relief because I knew that I would never be coming back this way again . . . NEVER!!

My decision to quit work seemed crazy—even to my family and church—because as a fairly senior Government Officer I was earning a healthy salary and I was guaranteed holiday pay and pension security. I would be nuts to leave all that behind wouldn't I? In the office peoples' reactions varied from disbelief to annoyance; while every time my mum looked at me I could see the disappointment and genuine perplexity on her face. (From time to time an elected family member would be tasked to come round and give me the talk, you know, the talk that would bring me back to my senses and force me back to normality!)

And they were right, in a way: it would have been much easier to stay in the job, after all, that's what most people do. Yet deep down in my soul there was a stirring, an alarm, an overwhelming prompting that I had to breakout—to be free! I knew that the "bus" on which I had been journeying successfully through life was no longer going my way and if I stayed on... It was going to crash My vision was beginning to develop and I began to see a different kind of life for myself; what I saw was a million miles away from the life I was living actually experiencing at the time, and I knew it was only a dream – just my imagination it felt so real!

In February 2004, Les Brown, the International Motivational Speaker came to my church. Whilst he was presenting to us I had a weird experience; it was as if what he said was a crystallization of all that I had been feeling. I felt transfixed. I had butterflies in my tummy; and a strong sense of knowing that I would be a world class Motivator speaking to crowds of people too!

Les told us to write down the things that we wanted in life. This was the first time that I'd ever thought about listing all the things that I'd been dreaming of. Something happened on that day, I conceived hope! I've still got that 5X7 card, and everything I wrote on it is slowly coming true in my life.

At the end of his presentation, our eyes met, we shook hands and these words came out of my mouth – completely bypassing my brain! I said, "Thank you for your presentation, I believe I'll share a platform with you one day!" He smiled, and said, "Well then, I should look out for you then!" He walked off, but then stopped short, turned around and said, "What is your name, young lady?" I told him and he said, "I'll be watching out for you." (I hope he's still looking out for me, because I'm on my my way!)

I was on a high all of that day, but it wasn't long before reality hit. I was in debt, struggling with failing relationships, raising Bianca by myself and really fed-up with my job. I was in the wrong place, but I had no clue about how to make to the transition to where I wanted to be. I was caught in a web of other people's expectations and my own fear—I was hooked on the certainty of the money's being there and couldn't see a way to survive without it!

I didn't realise it at the time, but I was also surrounded by emotional walls that I had spent most of my life erecting; walls composed of achievements, good grades, and a successful career, (achieving by the world's standards!). As I built my little empire I was also building the walls of self- sufficiency and independence so that nobody could get near enough to hurt me and reject me. I realize now that I had major issues, baggage that I was carrying around with me and I could feel them getting in my way: Legacies from hating the way I looked (I was born with a facial disfigurement)—such as being partly raised by a grandmother who never made any secret that I was her least favorite; from my father having left home, leaving me feeling hugely rejected. In fact, rejection and insecurity had been what my life had been about.

It was in the harsh wilderness time after leaving my job that I began to finally realise that my position, my accolades and my property portfolio gave me no sense of fulfilment anymore. Then brick by brick, certificate by certificate, my little empire came tumbling down around me!

It was the loneliest time of my life. I spent months in my dressing gown trying to uncover what my life was really about and. Because there was a shortage of people who could really identify with my radical leap of faith, I felt cut off from others and It was also a tough ride for my daughter, Bianca too, she had to "do without", though she never complained and always seemed to have a word of encouragement to build my faith!

Still, guilt and doubt sometimes threatened to overwhelm me, and I might even have turned back had it not been for the countless little miracles and blessings that showed up in my life, little sign-posts that suggested "Don't give up!" For example, we never went to bed hungry: miracles happened, food would turn up, money would turn up . . . And gradually during 2006 I discovered a new sense of purpose; I entered into a season of clarity and understanding, through which I realized what needed to be done. I needed to sell the house, clear my debt, and release the money I needed to invest in my vision – another huge step!

Basically I was now living what I had been learning. Ultimate success is more than money and position – It's about finding and becoming the best you can be no matter what you are doing. It is understanding that abuse, negative energy, destructive relation-ships or what ever you have been through are not strong enough to determine our future *unless we allow them to.* Even more: I had accepted that the universe is an awesome God-given creation that serves mankind by responding to our thoughts and desires. Learn-ing this helped me to break through my fears and to respond to the inner passion that emerged from my vision and mission to motivate the world to align their work life with their God given purpose.

We need to be open and clear-eyed to the potential inside us. Not long after I took the leap of faith to sell my house, I dared to set up a three-city Seminar tour, from which emerged two very important things. First, I learned that I really could impact people's lives. And secondly: I met a friend who told me about a dynamic new moti-vational speaker called Johnny Wimbrey! a student of Les Brown's! When a few weeks later I learned that Mr. Wimbrey was coming to town I signed up straight away! The law of attraction was at work!

To cut a long story short, when I saw Johnny and heard him speak

I was blown away with his power, sincerity and conviction. I spent that weekend following him around London, signing up for everything that he was selling! Somehow I just knew that I was meant to connect with this man: I had to. And now, almost a year on, I am co-authoring a book with Johnny! —He's a friend I feel privileged to have in my life. The law of attraction was working for me. So . . . what activates this law? In my case it was a heart to BE and the heart to GIVE and not the mind to RECEIVE that activated the law of attraction.

I believe that it works when you commit to do what you were created to do.

It works when you seek true success: when you find and develop the real you; and seek to be the best you that you can be (wherever you are, whatever you are doing and whoever you are doing it with! – Including WORK!)

It works when you develop powerful insights and revelations about who you really are and what God's purpose is for you. I discovered that what I have always loved to do and what I did really best was to bring transformation and truth to people's lives. This is my passion and as soon as I accepted it my imagination ran wild with ideas and inspirations about how I could use this passion and purpose to change the world!

I'm so glad now that I took the steps I did, even though they have been difficult to take. Now I'm doing what I truly love to do and getting paid for it. I'm flowing in my purpose – I don't believe we can be truly fulfilled till we flow with our unique purpose, gift and talents – when I'm doing what I'm doing I feel like I'm on wheels!

Now I'm committed to being the real me in and out of the workplace I see the Law of attraction operating all over my life. Sometimes it's spooky the way the answer or solution I'm looking for just presents itself! When I first began to have dreams and visions about speaking and inspiring people all over the world to recognise, grow and develop their unique purpose, I was actually mobilising the law of attraction in my life without knowing anything about the Law of attraction! I would spend hours meditating on the scenes of my future, I would weep with the passion I felt as I saw people being released into the truth of who they really are (still do). What looked from the outside like all hell breaking loose in my life was actually the labour pains that birthed me into a life of purpose.

I am convinced that my decision to step out of that job back in 2004 is one of the most powerful reasons why my life is the way it is today! —and that my experiences were a prerequisite for the work I am doing now. Of course, I still have a long way to go but I can tell you that, with God's help, my purpose has power. I now have a vision that dominates my life: I imagine a world where we are actively taught and encouraged to connect with our purpose and potential in the marketplace and we simply flow in it. That's why Unlocking Potentials my company came about.

It's definitely not an easy road and things can get rough; recently I set myself a challenge to walk home from church, maybe a 5-mile journey. At first it was easy but by the time I got to the last mile I was tired out; yet the thing that struck me the most about this experience was that it seemed like such a short, quick and easy journey in the car but actually walking it – I noticed – the roads that seemed ever so short and insignificant when in my car seemed long and interesting; I saw houses and shops that I had never noticed before; basically, I got a completely different understanding of that route!

I think living a life of growth and development is like that – we sometimes think about the moves we need to make and think we understand what it really takes, but the truth is we don't know until we step and walk it, for real. Thinking about it is like driving the car, its important to think but the growth results, rewards and rich life experiences come from actually walking it out.

I hope that as you read this you too are inspired to recognise that you have a unique contribution to give to your world, you can (and should) be using your job as another outlet in your life for expressing the truth of who you are. You should be loving going to work in fact it shouldn't be a chore, it should be a pleasure and lined up with you overall purpose. Purpose has a voice– It may be at this very moment calling out to you-- but if you get too busy with conforming then the voice of purpose can get drowned out. I am encouraging you to open your ears to the call of purpose on your life.

Working on living a life of purpose has been an amazing journey for me and I now understand that we are most useful to our world when we are doing what we were created to do, for me it is unlocking potential, because that's who I am, its what I bring to the table. Who are you? What do you bring to the table? I want you to think about how to be the real you in the world of work. You should be tapping into those gifts, qualities and passions that you were created with. Of course not all of us know who we are; but then, that's a whole other chapter!

Some questions to get you started

- Are you happy in your current position?
- What's *your* passion?
- Have you got issues preventing you from developing your potential?
- Are you living a life of purpose, on purpose?
- Are you asking yourself the right questions?

(Remember: The richest place on the planet is the graveyard – too many people go to their grave with the great contribution they were supposed to make on the earth firmly locked up inside!)

About the Author

Dion Johnson has more than twenty years' experience in health and social care, twelve spent as a midwife developing and managing services for teenage parents. After another two years in strategic management, Dion moved on to launch Unlocking Potentials, a consultancy created to reach people with her messages of hope and empowerment.

Dion's communication ability is enhanced by her experience as an overcomer. She was born with a facial disfigurement that set up patterns of poor self-esteem and rejection. Her life journey has been fascinating, and she brings it skillfully to her interaction with people. She is passionate about helping others to understand how to use adversity as a leg up to achieving their dreams.

Dion is trailblazing around the country as a speaker, employment coach, and personal development consultant with powerful seminars, motivational speaking sessions, and short courses that are stirring up a hunger for true success in the belly of today's people. To receive a pre-launch copy of Dion's new book, *Fed Up with Being Fed Up at Work!* log on now to www.fed-up-at-work.com or www.unlockingpotentials.co.uk.

Dreams Do Come True

Kalpesh Patel

*Carry your dream in your heart; if it is big enough,
it will carry you through the journey of attaining it.*

Imagine our lives are filled with miracles, if only we could see them all. I am blessed to have had a life filled with miracles, and every day I continue to experience life through this view; for this I am truly grateful. The story I wish to share will explain why I believe in miracles so strongly.

Over the years I have traveled the world training people, many who have shared their incredible stories of life's twists and turns, ups and downs, highs and lows; and all of them have contributed to me in their own ways, the effects of which cannot be measured, leaving their precious footprints all over my heart. There is so much I want to share with you about my life. In this short chapter I have chosen to share a series of events that have left me and my family in a state of continuing gratitude for God's grace. I hope to touch your spirit in a way that one day will serve you when you least expect it. May you will be empowered to always be the best you can be when life happens.

I believe that we are all born to contribute using our gift; all of us are born with a special seed that if nurtured will grow into something the world will benefit from. Mine is the gift of making a difference through my speaking, which flows through my life as oxygen flows through my lungs. The sad fact is that most of us get caught up in "circumstances" and forget how amazing we really are. I live to remind you of your greatness.

Most people are crushed by their first crush, left torn up by the opportunities, exams, and events they were going to tear up; they are shattered by the glass ceilings they were going to shatter, leaving them scarred and bitter rather than better. Every time we shrink back in life, our self-worth, self-esteem, self-image, and beliefs take a hard hit that most people do not recover from. We start playing safe, being average, and settling for mediocrity.

I hope to inspire you to stand up again and keep on going so that you can keep on growing. I believe we will never be faced with any event we cannot handle, that these events are in our lives to show us how strong, able, and gifted we truly are. This story is about an amazing couple who would change my life forever. Mum and Dad, I love you always. Thank you for everything.

I was fourteen years old, and when I came home from school, Mum sent me to see if Dad was okay; he had been feeling poorly all day. I ran upstairs to check on him, and he complained of pains in his left arm. That very morning we'd been taught in biology that this was a symptom of a heart attack, and I told him we should call the ambulance. He said not to worry; he would be okay. As the evening passed, he was not better, and something inside told me to make the call. The ambulance arrived and took Dad away. Mother went with him, leaving me to look after my little brother of twelve.

Later, Mum called and told me to call the family and tell them to come see him right away. We were a very close-knit family, where even our cousins were referred to as brothers and sisters. We had called the ambulance just in time. As soon as he had gotten to hospital, they had taken him straight to intensive care, where that night he would have three massive heart attacks. I still remember vividly thinking the worst. I was still a little boy, naïve and innocent. So scared of what would happen to us if dad were gone, I felt sick, coated in a cold sweat that would not go away. I remember being strong for my brother and mum, thinking that if the worst happened, I would have to step up and look after the family. That night was the longest night of my life. I just prayed and prayed for my dad and for strength. I had to be strong for them.

The following day we were all in the waiting room—uncles, aunts, cousins, me, Mum, and my little brother. The doctors called my mum out, and she was so strong; she came back a few minutes later, and without shedding a tear, she told us all that twenty-three doctors and student doctors had said that he was clinically dead. They had asked her for permission to switch off the machines. There was nothing more they could do.

She told the family to start a prayer in unison and asked the doctors for a few minutes alone with Dad. She had run out of a special ash she uses during prayer. As if by miracle, her brother had an envelope in his pocket with her name on it, and inside was the ash—unexplainable and, to many, unbelievable. I was there, so I had no choice but to witness the miracle.

Mum went in and prayed: "Dear Sai Baba, please give me my husband back, even if in a wheelchair for just ten years. Just until the kids grow up and can stand on their own two feet, they need their father." My mother is a very powerful woman, and what happened next was a testament to that. Doctors started running into the room, and it all looked chaotic to a fourteen-year-old; everything was happening so fast. Dad had come back. When the drama was over, the doctors came into the waiting room and told us all openly that they could not scientifically explain what had happened in that room in those few minutes. This was what we would call a miracle, God's miracle through the power of prayer and faith.

That night I grew up, and I made a promise to myself to look after my family always, no matter what. We had witnessed something that logic could not explain. The whole family grew that night. We grew stronger as a unit, and none of our lives would be the same again.

That was twenty-five years ago. I remember it like it was this morning.

My father was in the hospital recovering for what seemed like forever. Eventually he got a match for a heart transplant, one of the first few to have one in those days, at St. Bartholomew's Hospital, London. So much happened at that time, such intense feelings and emotions. None of it mattered, though—we got our dad back.

The following years flew by. Every day was a blessing, and we counted them daily. We never took life or each other for granted. Our love for each other and life grew stronger and stronger, and we would just be so happy together all the time. We would go for family walks every week, go to the gym together, eat together every evening, sharing stories and just appreciating each other. Health became a priority for us all. I would massage my mum and dad almost every night before going to bed. We had created a fairytale home.

We would hold weekly get-togethers with our extended family, where we would all connect spiritually and share stories. We valued every moment with each other and all the people in our lives. It was not just my father who had been given a new life; we all had been given that rare second chance.

Time flew by, and before I could count to ten, I was twenty-three, hugely successful as an individual and an entrepreneur, in love with my first love, and life was great. One evening at a family gathering, our doctor uncle told my mum's brother that Dad had little time left with us now. If he had any last wishes, we should fulfill them now. Doctor uncle was like a father figure to us all; he was very spiritual and had these insights, like a direct line with God. Dad had only one more wish: He wanted to see one of his boys get married. We both wanted to fulfill his dream. My twenty-one-year old brother was also in love with his first girlfriend, of three years. As it happened, my relationship was not to be—that is another story—but my brother was ready. The wedding was announced and would happen within three months.

We asked doctor uncle if we could delay because venues were not easily available, arrangements for the wedding would take time, and he said, do not delay even by one day. Time was too precious.

Three months later my brother had the most amazing wedding. It was a dream come true for us all, especially my father. He had his old friends and family fly in from all over the world—over 1,500 people showed up. Everything was perfect. Someone was definitely watching over us. As the wedding day neared the end, my father did not look well. He'd had a long day and lots of excitement, so we decided to take him home against his wishes. He always said he was fine; we knew otherwise.

That night he slipped into a coma in the hospital. It was the first weekend in May. His blood had gotten poisoned because his kidneys were failing him. The doctors said he must have been in excruciating pain the few weeks leading up to the wedding, but he had never said a word. His strength gives me power even today in dealing with life's challenges.

He stayed in a coma for the whole month, until he passed away that last weekend in May. You can never really prepare for the death of someone so close to your heart. My whole world shattered. I cannot explain the pain; it lived with me for a long time. My dad was my hero. He was my inspiration, and as a child I had wished I could be a fraction of who he was. I remember that I did not know how to handle my emotions. I felt trapped. I did not cry until the day they took the coffin away from the house; as they put it into the hearse, I let out a huge cry and broke down.

My father's death would change me for the worse.

I was sad that it was not me who had gotten married and made my dad proud. I had behaved like a self-centered idiot in those months running up to the wedding. I could have made it so much more meaningful for my family. We all go through tough times, and I was dealing with the rough times in my relationship and resented everyone for my failure. Just a few weeks after my father's death, I split up with the girl I had thought I would marry. We never really got that complete, and I never saw her again. The business went downhill. My mind was a mess, and I had no idea how to turn things around.

There were no classes in school or college on emotional intelligence. The Kalpesh before all this had been bubbly, happy go lucky, successful, and light-heartedly fun. I had been as optimistic as they get, always alive with energy. Now the flame in my eyes had been put out and replaced by sorrow and sadness. It wasn't long before this turned to anger, resentment, and bitterness. I blamed everyone and everything. I even blamed God. I forgot about the miracles and was focusing on myself. My relationships with my mother, brother, and sister-in-law were deteriorating, and the promise I had made a decade ago of looking after my family was forgotten.

I was destroying everything that was precious to me, and I lived as if my life were not worth living. This was my way of punishing God, of getting my own back in my twisted and distorted world. I hated God for what had happened. I would no longer be the best I could be; I would be the worst. I remember being so confused. My beliefs and my actions did not match up; who I was and who I was being were complete opposites. I'd cry myself to sleep many nights, not knowing how or if I would get my old self back.

A couple of years passed slowly until one evening I was invited to a seminar that would be another turning point in my life. The speaker talked about possibility, potential, greatness, and taking responsibility for our results in all areas of our lives. He shared his life experiences and how he got through them with power because of the books he had read and the self-teaching he had put himself through.

I was inspired by his sharing, and a flame was reignited inside of me. Things started making sense in my mind—events, decisions, actions—the clouds began to clear, and I could see things differently. I still felt lost as to how I would turn things around, but I saw light. I knew change was possible, and that was enough. It took an outsider, a complete stranger, to jolt my reality. That night I could not sleep. I was given a book called *Think and Grow Rich,* by Napolean Hill, and I could not put it down.

I decided to start taking responsibility for who I was and all my actions and results. This gave me power in the present. I felt alive again; a renewed energy entered my body. I was ready to snap out of my world of self-pity and sadness. I was consciously improving my thinking and re-evaluating my beliefs about myself and life. A new array of possibilities opened up. I almost had to force myself to smile again, be polite, friendly, warm, loving, generous—unlearning all the behaviors I had gotten used to over the last two years that had me trapped in a mindset that was keeping me down.

This was the beginning of my journey into self-discovery and personal development. I went on to read hundreds of books, watch all the videos, and buy all the audiotapes. I attended as many seminars as possible in as short a time as possible. The impact of compressed learning and fully immersing myself in this new information was unbelievable. My life went from strength to strength; my relationships with family and friends started blossoming; and my results went through the roof. I reprogrammed my mind with a new set of beliefs and values that were integral to successful people, and lo and behold, the results followed over the next few years.

To this day I still derive the benefits through my ongoing growth and development. The most important lesson I learned was that knowledge alone is not power; the application of knowledge is where the power lies. So many people know it all and have no results to reflect their knowledge. I repeated the learning, always trying to understand myself, who I was, how I operated and made decisions, and so on. Within a few days I saw my attitude shift, and in just a few weeks, my thinking and actions took on a new identity. A few months later, my results were reflecting my inner work. I got so much clarity on the distinctions of life skills that I could now teach and train others to be more effective in resolving life issues and challenges, helping them to get focused, find their passion, contribute more, be present to gratitude, and achieve personal success, whatever that was for them. This why I understand that *success is a choice*, and now I train people in the skills of success in my seminars all over the world.

I choose my reality consciously as events happen in my life, choosing powerfully the best possible thoughts, and this is due to the disciplined training I have put myself through over the years. You see, what was once a bitter experience is now a better experience. The way I see it now, my father died to go to a better place, and this pushed me to my darkest hour, where I would grow into who I am today. I know he sees all our progress and success, and he is proud of the legacy he left behind in his family. He watches over our every win and lives in our hearts as fresh as the day he was born.

Had I not gone through that pain, maybe, just maybe, I would have settled for average, a life of mediocrity, taking life for granted, never finding my passion or purpose. I thank God for my journey. Every day I dream of leaving this world a better place by touching as many lives as possible, transforming just one person at a time; if we all just did a little, we could change a lot. I travel the globe learning as much as possible about people, cultures, beliefs, and patterns. The bonus is that I grow through seeing more, by having a global perspective on life. I meet amazing people and I get to see this beautiful world we live in, building friendships, relationships, partnerships, leadership, and ultimately familyship.

I live to be used up in making a difference, sharing my views and experiences. I am a vessel for transformation and God's instrument for reaching people, integrating them to their spirit, the core of who they are. Today I have the honor of speaking all over the world in corporations, schools, colleges, universities, business seminars, and personal development seminars. I have had the privilege of speaking to over 300,000 people in the last decade. I am driven by my purpose of making a difference and my passion for achieving success. As for the future, God only knows. I have big dreams that I know will carry me if my legs ever get weak. My life is God's gift to me. Sharing it is my gift to you.

I am grateful every day I wake up to my parents for giving me a solid foundation to build my life upon and for the home they provided, which was filled with love, discipline, abundant thinking, and possibilities. My father always said that he hoped one day that his boys would live the dream, drive the cars, travel the world. Today his dreams have come true, and more important, so have ours.

I dedicate this, my first published work ever, to my mum and dad, who always encouraged us to be, do, and have everything good that life has to offer; they are everything a child could dream of.

Remember, life is never as bad as it seems. There are always people worse off than you, and it always gets better if you get better.

About the Author

Kalpesh Patel was born in Kenya and is of Indian origin. He grew up in London and was blessed to have amazing parents who where mentally wealthy regardless of financial challenges. Kalpesh is a dynamic and inspirational speaker who has touched more than 300,000 lives over thirteen years. A natural-born entrepreneur, he started out selling Coca Cola to fellow students at age eleven.

He attributes his success to his love of transforming lives and his winning attitude, which he inherited from his parents. Because he has overcome tough challenges, his friends and family say he is lucky, but he says, "We are all lucky if we are open to luck."

Kalpesh has walked away from an income of fifteen thousand pounds per week (yes, per week) to start again from scratch with Success University. Why? Because twelve years ago, personal development transformed his life forever. Now he can get paid for doing what he loves most, empowering others to be the best they can be. For more information, please visit www.thekalpeshpatel.com or call 0044 7956 436 703 (UK).

Conquering the Silent Demon Within

Phil Joyce

I opened my eyes after a night of disturbed sleep, teenagers coming and going late into the night. Thoughts about all I had to do at work had rushed through my head all night long. What would happen to the new police station design? What would I do about the performance issue facing me tomorrow? Would the budget bids be completed in time for Treasury? Would the bids get me more resources? What is the next step of this investigation and that investigation? When will the newspapers get hold of it? Has the minister been properly briefed? Where do I find the money to get my own executive assistant? How can I more effectively manage my workload and email traffic to keep from being constantly swamped?

I was exhausted before I had even started the day.

I turned over and my heart sank. I had slept in. It was already 7:30 a.m. By this time I was usually well on the road, traveling the 100 kilometers between my home and my office in Canberra, the capital of Australia. I felt defeated, lost, unable to move. I turned over and fell asleep.

The next day I arrived at the office at the usual time: 8:10 a.m. I wasn't feeling very well but greeted everyone who had started at 8:00 a.m. with the usual smile. There were more people here than last week. People had started to return from Christmas leave.

I quickly said hello to everyone, including my chief executive's executive assistant, Raewyn. She greeted me with a warm smile because it had been some three weeks since I last saw her. She had a look of concern in her eyes but I didn't stop to think about it. Instead, I headed into my office. My desk was clean and tidy, but my in-tray was already overflowing with ministerials, papers to sign, and submissions to read. There were red folders to clear before they went to the department's minister, because at the time, not only was I doing my own job, but I was acting deputy chief executive as well.

I settled at my desk feeling very sick. My mind was running at a thousand miles an hour. I experienced something close to dread as I pondered what I needed to do first, what tasks I needed to tackle, and fretted about what emergency or crisis I would have to manage that day. As an executive director reporting directly to the chief executive of a large and diverse department, my role crossed over every area of the department as well as across government. Consequently, I was used to getting more than 130 emails a day. And without a full-time executive assistant, I was having trouble managing my email traffic while shuttling between the six or seven long meetings I attended daily.

My stomach began to churn. I felt my face become hot and flushed, and my chest tightened. One day away from work, with half the department's staff still on Christmas leave, and I already had forty emails.

When I had left my office on December 21, 2007, for a short break over Christmas, I knew I hadn't addressed the 140 emails still in my inbox. They had played on my mind over the break, because I knew some were very important, especially the last one, which I had read before I left. It was a direction from Treasury to have a report on the auditor general's review of the department's financial statements completed by January 4, 2008.

Now, returned from my Christmas break, I saw messages about IT problems, messages about personnel problems, messages about procurement problems, messages, messages, messages filled with problems, problems, and more problems. I closed my eyes and couldn't bring myself to open even one email. I felt removed from myself, floating, looking about me as if in a dream. I put my head in my hands. What to do, what to do! A noise brought me back. I looked up and saw Raewyn. The concern that had previously shown only in her eyes was now etched all over her face. "Are you OK, Phil?" she said. Am I OK? No, not really, I thought. All I wanted to do was burst into tears, but I didn't. I said, "No, not really, Raewyn. I feel ill. I am going to clear the urgent things in this tray and go home." She looked concerned, told me to see her if I needed anything, and left.

It took me an hour and a half to clear those things that were urgent. I then left in a hurry, not wanting to make eye contact with anyone for fear of losing it. I waited anxiously for the lift, hoping that it would hurry up before someone caught me. The bell rang, and the door opened. I got in quickly; the lift looked old and tired even though it had recently been refurbished. I pressed the button for the basement and the lift started moving downward. It felt like it was dropping too fast. My head was spinning again as I hoped that the lift wouldn't stop at some other floor, forcing me to talk to someone.

I was in a dream hurtling toward the ground. I loved my work. What was happening to me? Finally, after what seemed like eternity, the lift told me I was on the basement level. The doors opened, and I moved quickly to the only sanctuary I had, my car. Get me out of here, my mind was saying, get me out. I drove into the sunshine and burst into tears. Not yet, not yet, people will see you when they come out of our building. Not yet, not yet. Keep face; don't let anyone see you crying.

I headed into the stream of traffic on the main road out of Canberra heading north. I can't do this job anymore, my mind kept telling me, I can't do it. The tears started rolling down my cheeks. My tears then became a flood. Cars were all around me, lights turning red, brakes on, stopping. People will see me, I thought. I need to stop crying. I can't. I must. I did—for a while at least.

The road from Canberra to Goulburn is dual lane all the way. Just as well, because I don't remember the trip other than the sobbing and the tears streaming down my face. I arrived home an hour or so after leaving the office. It was school holidays and the kids had some friends over. Gail, my wife, was in the kitchen. She looked up when I came in. "Oh, you're home early," she said

"Not well," I said and headed for our bedroom. I got changed and slumped onto our bed. My head was bursting; I had pains in my chest. I lay there staring blankly at the white ceiling. My eyelids grew heavy, and my eyes sunk deep into my head. I slept.

Later that evening I went to a medical clinic to see the afterhours duty doctor to get a medical certificate for yesterday and today. He gave me a certificate for the whole week. "Thank goodness!" I said, sighing. "I can have a rest." But the week went too fast. I slept a lot and did some pleasant things with the family. The surreal feeling that I had been experiencing had gone, but I was still very tired and had to tell myself continuously not to think about the weeks to come. The emails, the nagging people, the continual need to make effective decisions were constantly in the back of my mind. I had to tell myself to relax, for this week at least. I refused to listen to my own inner talk, seeking answers to the many questions that circled through my mind. It was a week to relax, and relax was what I must try to do.

Gail had taken one of our kids to see a naturopath the day after I had come home and had mentioned that I was suffering from stress. He told her that if I needed anything or simply someone to talk to, I should give him a ring. I listened to her advice but didn't do anything about it.

Monday soon arrived. My eyes opened wide. I hadn't slept well because the questions that had been circling my mind over the past week had now taken over. My head felt heavy against my pillow. I rolled over and stared at the clock sitting on the bedside table—5:30 a.m.—and my heart sank deep into my chest. Soon I would be up and getting ready for my long, now dreaded day at work. I tossed and turned and eventually got up and made my way to the kitchen. Gail and our children, Stuart, Rachel, Richard, and Sarah, were all peacefully sleeping. What I would have given to be able to have just one peaceful night's sleep.

Halfway into the hour drive I started feeling anxious. It was another week. More people would be returning from leave, including my boss, some of my managers, and my counterparts across government. My knuckles started to turn white. My fingers gripped the steering wheel as if I were fighting for control of the car. I could feel the same sense of surrealism flowing through my body. My head was pounding, my heart racing. My mind was telling me I couldn't do the job. Tears were pouring down my face, and my vision was blurred. There were cars all around me. The truck behind me was getting closer, my mind was wandering, I couldn't focus, the cars were speeding past me, I had to stop, I had to stop! Where to stop, where to stop?! I couldn't see the road properly. I pulled my car off onto the side of the road and stopped abruptly. My body was shaking. "Don't let people see you crying, What to do, what to do? Who to call? I need help. Who to call? Gail, Stuart, my mum, my brothers. Slow down your breathing or you will pass out, slow down, think; no I can't."

My twin brother, Michael, answered the call. "What's wrong?" he asked.

"I can't go to work. I'm on the highway, and I need help," I blabbered into my phone, still trying to stay strong and not break down in his ear, but it was no use. He told me that he would come and get me on the highway, but he had to get his son to school. I told him that I would make it to his place.

I had one more call to make. I needed to let them know at work. With tears streaming uncontrollably down my face, I shakily dialed my own work number, hoping that someone I trusted would answer the phone. My hopes were realized. I hadn't seen Tracey for four weeks. It was her first day back at work. I took a deep breath, tried to stem the tears to sound normal as I told her who it was. When she heard me, I could hear her voice relax as if talking to a friend rather than a business associate. I quickly told her that I would not be in today and ended my call. Not a nice thing to do to someone you respect, but I couldn't control myself anymore.

I eventually made my way to my brother's house in the southern suburbs through one of the worst traffic jams I have seen in Canberra. It took me nearly an hour. He greeted me with a smile, and then I really broke down.

I sat in his lounge room totally defeated, heavy with emotion, crying again for no reason, my head thumping, while Michael contacted the mental health crisis team. I could hear him giving the person on the end of the phone my symptoms. Was I suicidal, they asked. "No," I heard Michael say. "He loves his family too much to be that way."

Time stood still for many hours while he contacted Gail and Stuart, and they drove to Canberra to pick me up. I was totally dysfunctional, not able to string a sentence together, not able to think, just very, very tired and in a dream only I was living.

I needed help, but from where? We drove home in silence along a road that was as familiar to me as the back of my hand, yet I have no recollection of that journey. All I wanted to do was to sleep, sleep and forget, forget what had happened, but I knew I would have to face this silent demon again at another time.

Learning to Live in the Moment

This is a true story of executive burnout. And even though my breakdown happened three months ago, I am still suffering, still feeling anxious as I recall what happened to me. I have had a couple of serious setbacks, caused by an inability to manage simple day-to-day activities. Ordinarily I would have had no trouble in handling these, but this illness has reduced my capacity to manage more than one thing at a time. Strangely, only hours after suffering these panic attacks, I felt fairly reasonable. This illness does that. It plays with your emotions. But then when I tried to get back to my everyday life, even gradually, I felt far from reasonable. Let me tell you of one experience.

A friend had asked me to attend a six-hour-long information session on her behalf. I thought I was up to it. The day arrived. It was a Monday. I woke up feeling anxious and wasn't sure why. I showered, had breakfast, and got dressed. Time started to disappear, and my anxiety started to grow. I could feel myself getting nervous. Why was this happening? It was only a meeting, something I was used to doing routinely. I had to leave. I passed by the phone. Stopped. I couldn't do it. I rang my friend and told her I wasn't going. She was OK with it, but I felt I had let her down. I put the phone down, and then it happened. *Panic.*

I ran down the hallway ripping at my clothes. I had to get out of them, had to get rid of them. I couldn't handle it. I tried desperately to get my suit off, but I couldn't do it. Where was Gail? I needed her. She came quickly. She tried to undo my shoes. I couldn't get them off because I was still ripping at my shirt. The panic was all around me, the room was closing in. The kids, hearing my cries for help, had arrived in our bedroom. At last I was out of those clothes, but still I was not safe. I backed into our en suite, arms wrapped around my body, not knowing where to go. I crouched in the corner. "Rachel needs to get to work, Rachel needs to get to work," I repeated. I had planned on taking her on my way to the meeting.

Gail calmed me down and got me back to bed. I lay there, yet again, wondering why this was happening.

The mind is a powerful thing. We all know that, but until you experience such events as I have, you really don't appreciate how powerful it is. When I confided with my psychologist about this panic attack, I learned that although I thought it had come out of the blue, it hadn't. It was if all the planets had lined up to remind me that I wasn't out of the woods just yet. The day of the meeting was a Monday, the day I had first felt unwell and stayed at home. The date of the meeting was April 14, three months exactly since I had felt unwell and stayed home. It was the first day in three months I had put on a suit, one of the ones I always wore to work. The meeting agenda had items on it that I had no knowledge of, something that I always made sure I had before attending such things at work. I was going into an unknown environment with many people I did not know. It would have been the first "official" function I had attended since my collapse. While I didn't know it at the time, my brain was again saying to me, "You are not ready to do this, so I am not going to let you." Powerful, isn't it?

Although revisiting these experiences causes me pain, I hope that they provide some comfort to those who read this chapter. While the experiences were and still are the worst things I have had to endure, there is hope. If the brain can make you think and feel the way I did, then with help and support, the brain can help you gather strength and the will to recover—the will to conquer this silent demon within.

You know, the most pressing issue I faced when this happened three months ago was my feeling of failure, the honest belief that

I had let everyone down, especially my wife and children. I have always tried hard to provide for them, to be successful to ensure they have a good and happy life. I have also tried to teach our kids that, in life, you need to strive to be successful, not wait for success to come to you. I tell them they have to go out and find whatever their passion is, set their own limits, and endeavor to be the best they can at whatever they choose.

Gail and I are not overbearing parents. We believe you have to do what you want to do to be happy. So we do not try to influence our children with what we might want them to do, but we give them choices from which they can make decisions and learn from their experiences.

Our kids are great. They are well respected and independent of thought, have wonderful friends, and get on with each other—well, usually. Helping them grow up, respecting their choices, and seeing them grow into exceptional people has been a very special time for both of us. I feel that they look up to us for how we have raised them. But one of my initial overwhelming fears in conquering this illness was what they would think of me now. I know they won't be able to ignore how differently I am acting. I am home each day rather than rushing out to work and having only about three hours a day to be with them. I know that seeing me like I am, sometimes in total despair and breaking down in front of them for no obvious reason, isn't what they want, and it's definitely not the way I want them to see me. I have always been able to control my emotions. But you know, no matter how hard I tried, I couldn't pretend to be my old self in front of them, even though I was in my own house, which was my only true sanctuary.

I was unsure about whether I should talk to them about what had happened or how it had happened and whether such a talk would make any real difference in their understanding of my behavior. They are still fairly young, the eldest, Stuart, being nearly twenty; Rachel, seventeen; Richard, fifteen; and the youngest, Sarah, almost thirteen. Would they truly comprehend what had happened to me, when I had gone from being part of a senior executive team in a high-profile department to someone who couldn't stop crying, someone who couldn't control himself? How was I going to get through this if they didn't understand that unlike a person with a broken bone, I was injured and sick even if I didn't look like it? How would I get through this without gaining their support? But children have this unique ability to recognize things for what they are. My fear of failing them was of no concern to them, because in their eyes I hadn't. They were simply happy to have me at home. In fact, Richard and Sarah have said many times since, "This thing that happened to you has been great for us. We enjoy having you around us more often. We enjoy having you drop us off and pick us up from school. We enjoy being able to go down to the shops with you. We enjoy just being with you."

Now, if that isn't the most magical healing potion, I do not know what is.

Their support and their acceptance that their father has had a nervous breakdown is breathtaking and very humbling. They love me for simply being me, not for who I am in other people's eyes.

The lesson from my family has been to live for the moment. I never really did that. I was constantly planning our future, the department's future, considering all the risks, and navigating through the politics for a better result. I can't imagine why that was so important now. Of all the lessons I have learned through this experience, the importance of living for the moment is the most profound.

Let me give you an example.

Not long after I collapsed, Stuart, who had started a laser skirmish (tag) business not long beforehand, was having a group come to our property on the weekend. He needed some paths cut through some of the bush on our ten acres. While he had started, there was still more work to be done, so I went outside to cut back some of the overhanging bush.

The evening air was cool, with a light rain falling, soft enough that you could feel it against your face as if tiny fairies were flapping their wings against your cheeks. The trees moved gently as a light breeze rustled their leaves and the sunset slowly faded to grey. I was feeling nice and warm, rugged up in a new laser skirmish jacket, clippers in hand, as I slowly cut my way through the myriad blackberry bushes, stems, and branches of this overgrown area of our forest, as we call it. The feeling of peace and tranquility was so strong that I just marveled in my own existence, the beauty of it all, the misty rain, the smell of the bush, the earthy scent of the dampened ground, the sounds of native birds settling down to rest for the night. What had brought me to this moment? Why had I been given this chance to simply exist and be one with nature? I began to pray, something that I had not done for many years. I had a sense of absolute oneness with the world, with God, and with myself. It was and is one of the most spiritual and powerful experiences I have had in my life.

Here's another.

My illness has given me a desire to walk. I find it very therapeutic. One day I was out walking and some close friends, Bob and Jane, drove past on their way out to Bob's farm. They stopped and invited me to go with them to see Bob's recent building project. We arrived at Bob's house and inspected the new outdoor living area. I was very impressed.

A year earlier Stuart and I had helped Bob by mowing an area of his yard that was well and truly overgrown. I turned around to see what he had done with it and got a very pleasant surprise. Its boundary was now displaying a splendid array of yellow and red roses, neatly planted in well-maintained garden beds. At the end of the yard stood a magnificent grove of Australian eucalyptus trees. I walked down to have a closer look when Bob came up behind me and said, "Come with me. I want to show you something." He took me to one of the bigger gum trees and told me to take a look at it. He then said, "You know, Phil, this is a very special moment that has been made only for you. Look at the new growth on this tree, its colors, the light breeze moving through its leaves. If this moment has been made for only you by God, a moment to marvel at Mother Nature's splendor, why would He let anything happen to you that was not good for you?" Powerful words. That moment was something that I never would have experienced if I had not had this breakdown.

So my advice for those of you reading this book is to live for the moment. Take time out of your busy day and look around you. You will be amazed. Revel in the ingenuity of the human race, marvel at the inventiveness and creativity of Mother Nature. Recognize that no matter what you do or who you are, you are unique, someone who, no matter what happens to you, deserves to be here, deserves to be respected, deserves to be happy. You deserve to believe in what you believe, to believe in the intangible, to love and be loved. Savor the moment.

Self-Discovery

I often wonder how my illness affected my work colleagues, because my departure was very quick. As I mentioned earlier, I felt that I had let many people down. This feeling extended to my colleagues and staff, especially my boss. The feeling of letting her down was so strong that I was not able to communicate with her or see her for many, many weeks. I couldn't contemplate looking her in the eye, although I needed to see her to explain, but I couldn't bring myself to do it. So when the opportunity presented itself through third parties, I sent a message saying I was sorry for deserting her. Eventually I forced myself to travel to Canberra to have coffee with her and Tracey, who had taken my call when I had collapsed on the side of the highway. We arranged a meeting well away from the office, because even to this day I am unable to face the thought of walking back into my building, standing in the lift, and walking through that door to my office. The absolute fear turns my stomach.

I have tried to rationalize why I felt like I had let everyone down, especially my boss. With the support of my naturopath and my psychologist, I have come to realize that my feelings were actually a grieving process that I had to go through to distance myself from a work obsession that had all but consumed me. I had crossed over that thin line where work is work, and where time for me and my family should be just that, time for me and my family. I needed to regain some balance, and my mind was helping me to do so.

The coffee meeting was not at all pleasant for me. I again made a fool of myself as I delivered my sorry message in person by crying, being edgy, and being very emotional. But it was the beginning of my healing process, because I started to realize that my feelings of failure were mine alone. People still had confidence in me, they still respected me, and they still liked me. They were feeling that they had in fact let me down by not recognizing that I was in trouble, by not being able to convince me at the time that I may need to slow down, to reprioritize my work, to seek help.

This revelation led me to consider how I had been behaving before my breakdown. Ordinarily, I am a happy-go-lucky sort of person, someone who brushes off obstacles as challenges, someone who frequently preaches the message: "Only consider those things over which one has control and forget the rest." I enjoy seeing others prosper, motivate my staff by recognizing their achievements, and provide opportunities for them to develop and grow so that they can move on and into better positions; I am someone who will do silly things and make a fool of himself for a good cause, like cross-dressing and running all over Canberra to raise much-needed funds for the Australian Red Cross.

I was always ready for a laugh. But in hindsight, and in listening to people close to me since my collapse, I had become withdrawn, not able to smile, consumed by my work, forgetful, irritable toward my wife and our children, unable to sit still, and always on the move, often awake at night thinking about work and even sending emails, never able to sleep in or simply enjoy the warmth of our bed on the weekend, losing my temper over an overrun on a capital works project, something I never did previously, refusing to acknowledge colleagues' concerns about how tired I was looking. All these signs were there, but I didn't stop, I didn't live for the moment, I didn't take time to consider any of these hints before my body simply said, "I have had enough," and I found myself unable to function.

Following my collapse, none of my staff was told what had happened to me, and I was not in any fit state to let them know. But slowly as the word got out, and after my coffee with my boss and Tracey, I found the strength to email all my managers and personal staff. Many of them returned my message with words of support and encouragement. They had been confused about what had happened to me and so were thankful that I had let them know. I found that when you are up front about depression and workplace anxiety, people treat you not as an outcast, as my original thinking had been, but with sincere compassion.

Many of those in whom I confided told me stories of depression and burnout that they or someone very close to them had suffered. I am amazed at how many people I know who have either suffered the illness or had someone close to them go through the same experience. Its prevalence has actually helped me recognize that it does not have the stigma it once had, that it is now recognized as an actual illness, and most important, that it is treatable.

Treatment

Treatment is a personal thing, however. Once I was diagnosed with depression and work-related stress, I was given a choice. My choice was influenced by many people: my family, my friends, my naturopath, my psychologist, the Internet, and the numerous doctors I saw before I could get in to see my regular GP. It is important that in making this choice about your treatment, you receive good advice.

When I suffered my second breakdown on the side of the highway, and following that harrowing trip back home, I was not able to get in to the doctor who had treated me the week before, so I took Gail's advice to see the naturopath. She arranged for me to see him after hours and then drove me to his practice. I was in no fit state. I was not able to think straight, not able to stem my embarrassment of continual crying.

When we arrived, he gently took me back to what had happened. He listened to me. He spoke of the need for me to take time out for myself, to recognize that I was injured, that I was depressed. It came as a bit of a shock. Me? Depressed? No.

I knew I was upset, but I didn't see myself as being depressed. Rather, I saw myself as overworked. Although I respected his advice, "the system" required that I see a doctor to get a sickness certificate for work. A few days later, I saw a doctor who was referred to me by a friend. He was very blunt about his prognosis and informed me that if I didn't do what he told me to do regarding a course of antidepressant drugs, I would be suicidal or be having shock treatment within six months because I was "too far gone."

I came away from that encounter very angry and very determined to beat my illness without the use of drugs. My determination was strong; my will to do it by myself was compelling. I told my family that this would be my goal. I simply didn't want to take drugs that would control my mind. I believed that the power of my mind would be strong enough to pull me through this, but I also recognized that to strengthen my mind, I needed psychological help. I saw another doctor and asked for a referral to a psychologist. While waiting for this appointment, I visited my naturopath on numerous occasions. He again listened to me and questioned me on how I felt, and together we tried to put the mental jigsaw together so that I understood what had actually happened to me. I enjoyed these appointments; he was making very good sense to me, speaking of such things as needing to set up a routine by which I could concentrate on only one thing, while putting other concerns away for a future time. Only then should I think about such things. He put me on a course of herbs to help me relax and sleep. They did a great job and helped me to settle myself.

I wondered what my GP would say about my "no drug" decision when I eventually saw him. While he was relaxed about my desire to beat this illness without any prescribed drugs, he cautiously hinted that my decision might need to be revisited. I remained on the herbal treatment for a month and half, and I really felt that with the assistance and support I was getting, my quest to beat the illness without prescribed drugs was on track. But progress was slow.

I tried focusing on something new and different to keep my once overactive mind alert. I helped my son with his new business, but there was too much to think about. While at work, I had dealt with twenty issues at once and made critical decisions every minute of the day, but my ability to be flexible in my thinking was gone.

With my emotions still very unstable and raw, I did not have the energy to think myself through this situation. My mind was not as strong as I wanted it to be, and I was getting pressure from Canberra to start considering a return-to-work program to assist me in extending my now depleted sick leave entitlements—pressure, of course, that I really didn't need.

I then suffered a number of events that took me from feeling OK to the depths of despair yet again. I was unable to control my emotions, whether in front of those I love or perfect strangers. My desire to beat the demon stirring deep within me without taking prescribed drugs came to a sudden end. I spoke with my doctor and psychologist about the effects of taking the medication. They both went through with me the various things that might happen and convinced me that it was for the best. I trusted them.

The initial week was not good for me. I was very tired and slept a lot, I had bad nightmares, I was irritable toward my family, my mind was constantly in a fog, and I was not a pleasant person. Yet the desire to get better, to be normal again, became my focus. I needed to smile and laugh once more. I needed to feel like my old self. This became my challenge. I persisted with the medication, supported by Gail, our children, my mother and brothers, my psychologist, doctor, close friends, and case managers.

Slowly I have felt myself getting better and stronger. The medication has given me some perspective that I did not have before. It has allowed me to watch TV and not cry at silly, emotionally driven commercials, for heaven's sake. It has allowed me to negotiate a return-to-work program that suits my present needs. It has allowed me to negotiate with banks and creditors about my inability to pay future mortgages and bills, as I will shortly be without any income while "the system" investigates my workplace injury claim. This is a sad indictment of our federal worker's compensation system, which only supports people who have enough personal leave to cover the four months it takes to investigate a claim. Under this system, my monthly income will be reduced to zero, while I still have to support our family of six. This is a system that I will try to influence and fix once I have recovered.

The thing about depression is that because it is so personal, and those of us who suffer from it experience it in so many different ways, treatment must be personalized. My experience with the doctor who told me that I would become suicidal was, to me anyway, an example of his experience stereotyping me. He did not take into account my own beliefs and values, did not make allowances for how I wanted to be treated. Yet the other health professionals who are treating me have allowed me to have a point of view, to try it on my own. Only when I realized myself that I couldn't do it did they guide me toward a suitable solution. This is effective support.

Although initially I was determined to recover without drugs, although I was absolutely against the idea of them and their side effects, I know that drugs have helped me. When it comes down to it, I am stronger than I was when I wasn't taking them. My family has seen a difference. I also know I am not seen as having failed in my goal to beat depression without drugs; in fact, people are congratulating me for taking the decisive step. Medication has allowed me to smile again, to enjoy life, to enjoy living for the moment. It has given me hope, knowing that I will beat this. It has given me the ability to laugh.

Losing your sense of humor because you have lost your will to achieve or to be motivated or to see the funny side of life is a tragedy. Humor is an essential element to being human; it drives creativity, fosters effective relationships, and improves communication and listening skills. How many times have you been down in the dumps only to be lifted by humor? Maybe someone tells a joke or you see something funny on TV like bloopers or funniest home videos and suddenly your dark day is brightened.

Humor, like exercise, stimulates the brain and can be effective treatment for depression. In the early stages of my illness, I lost my sense of humor. I lost the ability to smile and laugh, something I longed to regain. In fact, I discussed this with our daughter Rachel, who is always laughing and joking around, often about herself. We spoke about my inability to be happy, to simply see the funny side of things happening around me. We talked about my inability to realize that things would improve, that "this too will pass."

As the weeks turned into months, humor became important to me. I started to seek out people with a sense of humor, even a wicked one. When I found these people, I relished our conversations, because sooner or later, I knew they would tell me one of their stories or simply say something that would make me laugh. They did, and the feeling was stupendous. To feel myself smile, to hear my voice break into the sound of laughter, to sense that wonderful feeling that I would split my sides from laughing was just the best medicine. Laughing lifts one's spirits, creates endorphins in your brain, and generates happiness. I couldn't help but remember the old adage, "Smile and the world smiles with you; cry and you cry alone." Of course, I wasn't always alone when I cried, but smiling and laughing definitely helped my recovery.

My story is one that hundreds of thousands of people around the world are telling. Depression caused by burnout is common. It doesn't matter if you are a highly paid executive or a mother or father looking after your kids. The important thing is that as soon as your body and your brain tell you that you can't do it anymore, you must do something about it. You must seek help.

This is why I jumped at the chance to tell my story when Johnny Wimbrey and Bobby Minor put out the call to be part of this book. It is my way of reaching out to those hundreds of thousands of people suffering what I have suffered and am still living through. It is my way of making a difference. I know that something positive can come from this traumatic time in my life.

The mental process of having to relive my experiences while writing about them has helped me put things into perspective. While it has been painful and exhausting, the process of putting pen to paper has been therapeutic. It has awakened a lost dream within me; it has reignited a lost desire to use my imagination, to write books, to visualize a time when I was happy, a time when I was a success, a time when I knew who I was and where I was going. It's also made me thankful for all I have learned from this experience. And finally, it's given me a new dream, a dream to help others suffering the same fate.

Although I don't know what will come of my career in government, I am now ready to take up again the challenge of seeking new directions, of chasing new dreams, of living for the moment, while at the same time conquering the silent demon within.

About the Author

Phil Joyce lives with his wife and four children in Goulburn, New South Wales, Australia. He has held numerous senior executive and management roles across government and the private sector: operational, marketing, and corporate roles in Australia's national airline Qantas; academic roles with the NSW Police Service, specializing in crash investigation, police driver training, and VIP protection; and senior executive roles within public service. His diverse background has led to interests in organizational development and change, marketing, human resources, education, training, strategic planning, and risk assessment. Phil has also consulted in the fields of organizational structure and effective leadership. He holds a masters of education, diploma in teaching, graduate certificate in management, graduate certificate in marketing, and Certificate IV in assessment and workplace training.

Helpful Links

- http://altmedicine.about.com/od/healthconditionsatod/a/Depression1.htm
- www.beyondblue.org.au
- www.beattheblues.info
- www.movember.com
- www.reachout.com.au
- www.depression.com
- www.executive-burnout.com (my own website soon to be launched)

Books

- Burns, David D. *Feeling Good*. New York: Avon Books, 1999.
- Marsh, Nigel. *Fat, Forty and Frustrated*. Sydney: Bantam, 2007.
- Meares, Ainslie. *Relief without Drugs*. London: Harper Collins, 1968.

Transcending Your Past

Angel Carr

An innocent little girl sits underneath the big tree near that old dirt road watching the beautiful sunset. The tears are quickly drying as they stream down her rosy cheeks, leaving a residue of pain and embarrassment because of what has just happened to her. She sits secretly recovering from what would repeat itself time and again throughout her life. Mothers don't watch as closely when children are supposed to be playing innocently with a friend. The girl's life was filled with hurt, abuse, and shame. She grew up remembering times when her mother would hide her from satanic cult members who had kidnapped her sister when she went to town one day. The girl shed many silent tears. Seeds were planted without her having a choice. That little girl was me.

We all have a past, but your past doesn't have to have you.

I was raised in a small town with a population of 1,300 people, only 3 to 5 percent of whom I could identify with. Coupled with my harsh life experiences, the small town upbringing didn't help my self-esteem in any way. Eventually I started playing sports, made the cheerleading team, and started enjoying life. Halfway through my cheering season, however, we moved to the city. I was crushed. There were more children in the new school I attended than in the entire town I came from. I dreaded the ride to and from school every day. The route seemed like an hour each way. I played sick as much as I could. In fact, I was sick—with fear of going to school and facing abuse from other children.

Being a country girl, I didn't fit in with the other kids. I spoke with a strong "proper" accent, and it was obvious that I wasn't from the area. I began to wonder how I would fit in there, or whether I would ever fit in. The clothes I wore were already out of style, not to mention my "little girl" hairdos. Where I was from, those things didn't matter much.

I would stand alone and wait for the bus, hoping the first seat would be empty so I wouldn't have to walk too far once I got on. I was the laugh of the bus each morning. I was miserable. My father stayed in my hometown to work because he could make more money. Therefore, my mom made provisions the best she could while living in Fort Worth. We had been an upper-class family in my hometown and had never wanted for anything until we moved to the city. My sisters ended up living with a relative in order to attend a high school in a better area, and later on, the rest of us moved in with the same relative for a while.

Unbeknownst to my mother and father, we were tormented daily. We couldn't sit here, couldn't sit there, couldn't eat this, couldn't eat that. We were told to get up and clean up whether anything was dirty or not. We were treated horribly. We would spend hours at night looking for clothes for the next day just to find the same outfit that we had worn a couple days prior. I vividly remember the sales Payless used to have on sandals—$9.99 for one, or two for $17.99. But even that was out of our reach. I used to want them every summer, but I didn't ask. I keep this in mind, to remember how far I've come. I was so glad when my father came and got us.

But the scars remained . . .

A few years after I married the man I had loved since I was ten years old, our marriage started falling apart. I was instantly a wife, mother, and stepmother at the tender age of nineteen. I hadn't mastered the role of a teenager, let alone developed the maturity for those other responsibilities. The little white picket fence began to lean, and the white house began turning shades of blue. It wasn't long before my husband, the chief provider, was forced to change jobs because the company he was working for moved to Mexico. His weekly pay was cut to approximately a quarter of what we were used to living on. The bills didn't change, and the financial responsibilities from before our marriage remained the same, but the net pay plunged severely. The world that I knew was coming to an end, or so I thought.

To say we were living from paycheck to paycheck is putting it mildly. We lived from day to day. We would wait for saving bonds to reach the six-month maturity to buy food and pay bills and oftentimes rent. I applied for emergency assistance but was denied because I drove a brand new car. Treading water was all we could do. I had gone from living a life of wealth and luxury to a life of lack. Life's obstacles had separated us into individuals who were more like roommates than a united couple. Depression began to settle in and take over my life. The world had stolen my joy.

I began looking for that joy and happiness in all the wrong places. I was incomplete and unhappy. I was constantly looking for validation, happiness, and acceptance. I was never satisfied with anything about me, including my weight (even though I was small), my hair, my face. I was satisfied with nothing at all. I made drastic changes to my hair, sometimes daily. Little did I know that I was searching for something that only God could supply. My husband couldn't help me because he was depressed, too—something guys don't talk about and sometimes think is impossible.

Frequenting clubs, dancing in videos, auditioning for other videos, and hanging out with friends became a way of masking my real identity. With the encouragement of my father, I enrolled in barber school and later received my Class A barber's license, but I remained unfulfilled. The fulfillment I found on my own was a temporary crutch that used to make me smile and get me through long sad nights and tough times, but it was also leading me down a path of destruction.

I began leaning on flesh instead of God, but that crutch was painfully taken from my life because *God is a jealous God, and there will be no other god before Him.* Anything or anyone we lean on or put above Him or in His place becomes our god. I was in the dry place of my life. I felt worthless! Reality set in, and I realized I was still incomplete inside, and no one could help me. But God keeps us even when the flesh doesn't want to be kept. This is when my life changed drastically, though unfortunately not for the better. Anytime there is emptiness, we find ways to fill that void. Some fill it with alcohol, drugs, promiscuity, or Jesus. It's your choice. I knew the choices I had, but I continued to make the wrong ones, blaming others for my unhappiness. I was also blaming my past for what I was doing. I kept sinking deeper and deeper into a bottomless pit. I would spend countless hours away from home, mainly at my mother's house, and finally late at night, I would start my journey home.

My path would take me by a cemetery, and I wanted so desperately to be there. The fresher the grave, the more I envied the person who had been laid to rest that day. In my mind, they had escaped this life. I was sane enough to know that I was in trouble to be thinking that way. Sometimes I would find myself almost or all the way home and never remember getting to that point. The tears would flow from how messed up I was and had been since I was a little girl. I carried secret hurt and pain that nearly destroyed me because I kept it inside and never shared it with my loved ones. The past that had been blocked out of my mind began to creep back to remembrance. I had hit rock bottom. I had had enough!

I was raised in a Christian home with wonderful parents, and they were my foundation. And I knew enough about God to make a conscious decision. I knew that He would make a change in my life if only I'd ask. So I did.

My life didn't change immediately, but I knew I had to make a choice. Yes, I was praying, but in my heart I wanted to give only the portion that I felt I couldn't handle instead of my whole self. We like to pick and choose what we want to give God, but that's not the way it works. We have to totally surrender. Many of us have a habit of believing that if we ask God to forgive us or come into our lives, we are immediately pulled out of our current troubles. That's not the case. Through the trials and tribulations, we learn our purpose, become stronger, pray, and exercise our faith. We have to go *through,* not around. If we're rescued prematurely from situations, the lesson is lost.

One thing I did know, hold on to, and take refuge in is the fact that nothing we can do will surprise our Father. That was reassuring. He told Jeremiah, "before I formed thee in the belly, I knew thee." I take comfort in knowing that He knew me before I was formed. And He throws our sins in the sea of forgetfulness. If He forgets them, why do we allow ourselves and others to hold us hostage to our past?

All things work together for the good of those who love the Lord
and are called to according to his purpose.
—Romans 8:28

What Am I Here For?

I started seeking purpose. I knew God had not brought me this far to leave me, and I knew there was a calling in my life. Had I not gone through trials and tribulations, I wouldn't be the woman I am today. To whom much is given, much is required. Therefore, sometimes we are held to a higher standard than someone else we see prospering (in our eyes), who lives worse than we do. For example, I expect more out of my elder son than the younger one. Even comparing them both at the age of ten, I expected more from the older one than the youngest, who was recently diagnosed as dyslexic.

I knew what my faith had brought me through. It was recommended to me to abort a pregnancy because of major complications while I was in my first trimester. A tumor was detected, and one of my doctors asked me which was more important—living to be a mother to my other two children or dying with the one I was carrying. Another doctor asked, "Where is your faith?" I chose to go through with the pregnancy and have the surgery the day I turned sixteen weeks. During surgery, three-quarters of my abdominal wall had to be replaced with an artificial mesh, and doctors weren't sure how it would respond to the next five and a half months of continuous growing. I had many months to lie flat on my back and pray. Five months later, my miracle was born healthy and strong.

I began fluently speaking the Word over my life because, after all, death and life are in the power of the tongue. I spoke life, prosperity, and other positive things into existence. I managed to further my training and education. Everything I needed to be successful was inside of me. I began letting go of the things that had reigned over me for so long. I replaced blaming with taking responsibility. I forgave when I didn't know I had not forgiven. Finally I understood that I couldn't change my past, but I could take the lead role in my future. My faith unlocked the deadbolts that were on my life.

Your life is your movie, and you decide who's the leading lady.

I began to speak over my marriage and over my children. I saw myself as whole and complete. I would rehearse self-building phrases until I believed them. "I am fearfully and wonderfully made; I am a phenomenal woman; I see myself the way God sees me. He made me in His own image." Above all, I became grateful for even the smallest things and gave to others even when I didn't feel I had anything to give. Giving opens doors. The psalmist says, "I will bless the Lord at all times; his praise shall continually be in my mouth" (Psalm 34:1). Praising confuses the adversary. I have learned how to be grateful for everything. I found a great quote by Melodie Beattie: "Gratitude unlocks the fullness of life. It turns what we have into enough, and more. It turns denial into acceptance, chaos to order, confusion to clarity. It can turn a meal into a feast, a house into a home, a stranger into a friend. Gratitude makes sense of our past, brings peace for today, and creates a vision for tomorrow."

When I changed my mindset and came clear on what I wanted my life to be, I started attracting people, books, CDs, and articles. I took a public speaking class, and the instructor spoke words of encouragement to me. Midway through the semester, after a presentation, she advised me to become a motivational speaker. I began practicing and improving that gift every time I had the chance. I watered those seeds with knowledge and positive speaking. Seminars that were once denied me became available. Leadership opportunities opened at work and at church. I began positioning myself for where I wanted to go in life. I started writing the vision because as I learned from *The Secret*, if I go there in the mind, I will go there in the body. Seeking and attracting individuals who could help me make my dreams come true was becoming a reality. Favor was upon me. I am blessed and am continuously being blessed exceedingly, abundantly above all that I could think or ask.

Through it all, I have been healed from self-esteem concerns. My marriage has been restored, my children are blessed, my business is taking a direction that I didn't know to ask for. And my little miracle is seven years old. The enemy of fear that holds us back from our dreams is no longer a part of my life.

I have a passion for helping hurting women with low self-esteem because I am a witness that it starts early in most cases. But I know you don't have to be what happened to you. I now use the gifts I have been blessed with to aid in cultivating individuals to find their purpose in life. Girl Talk, a ministry to build self-esteem and aid in self-validation and purpose-finding, was birthed from the years of pain I endured and what I learned from talking to friends with similar pasts and stories. I minister and teach women that true beauty comes from within the soul, which illuminates the face with a beauty that only the Master can give.

You are already equipped with every tool. After all, it starts with you, the person who looks back at you when you stand in front of the mirror.

> *No one can make you feel inferior without your consent.*
> —Eleanor Roosevelt

Success is partly defined by Webster as "The achievement of something desired, intended, or attempted." With that, I am successful each time I am able to plant seeds and watch the fruit of my harvest.

Dream Killers

Stay away from what I refer to as dream killers. That aged saying "misery loves company" is so true. I'm speaking of people who will say, "You can't do that" or "Do you know how much money and time that will take?" I'm also speaking of those who are silent dream killers. The unfortunate truth is, sometimes the dream killer doesn't know it's even happening. Just remember that your dream is *your* dream! It's not your father's, your mother's, your friend's, or anyone else's. It's yours.

I've learned to carry an umbrella for those who try to rain on my parade.

Oftentimes I am reminded of Joseph and his dream. His dream wasn't understood by his brothers because it was a dream given to him by God. His brothers sold him into slavery, put him in a pit, and did other nonbrotherly acts to him, but they couldn't deny his destiny. We have to be like Joseph and continue to keep our eyes on our God-given vision. As stated in the book of Philippians (1:6), "he which hath begun a good work in you will perform it until the day of Jesus Christ." This is just another way of saying that, no matter what goes on in your life, no matter what obstacles you come to, your ending is already decided. God has got your back!

About the Author

Working in the corporate world of higher education, Angel Carr has used her position as a stepping stone, a learning tool, and way of being a direct link for those who have been led her way. Angel has a deep compassion for building self-esteem and self-worth of individuals, especially young girls, teens, and women. She believes a healthy admiration for self contributes to attitude and altitude, which is why she founded Girl Talk for women, early teens to elder adults, where she shares information and helps women escape the many hats that they are forced and sometimes choose to wear. Recently she began heading the His and Hers Roundtable as a way of giving back and using life's experiences and mistakes to educate men and women in marriages and relationships. His and Hers Roundtable consists of married and single male and female adults with one purpose in mind—building lasting friendships and relationships.

Angel also volunteers her services as a licensed barber and stylist for nonprofit organizations, schools, and churches that help women and young men to develop confidence, skills, and knowledge. She works in particular with an organization that targets all ages of at-risk girls, welfare recipients, and single parents. Angel has been married for more than eighteen years, and God has blessed her and her husband with three wonderful children. She lives in Fort Worth, Texas, with her family. Visit her website at www.angelsalonsweet.com or contact her by email: cowgirlwithcurves@yahoo.com.

The Power of Faith, Hope, and Love

Jacklyn Ker

My grandmother's face flashed across my mind. I could see her eyes staring back at me. She looked like she wanted to tell me something, but I couldn't reckon what it was.

Then her image disappeared. I looked up.

The sky suddenly appeared vividly blue to me, and I was shocked. Why hadn't I noticed that seconds earlier? I must have been at least twenty stories high. The trees were green round balls below my feet. Cars were tiny colored rectangular boxes.

What am I doing here? I wondered. I had no answer, and I didn't have a single idea why I had put myself in such a dangerous position.

I retrieved my dangling leg from the railing and took off at top speed. That was probably the fastest I had run since my competition days. I felt scared. I was lost. I was in shock.

This was my first failed attempted suicide. Without knowing it then, I had already begun to make critical choices. I chose to live, but I regretted this choice—not once, but twice.

It was 1992, and I was twenty-six years old.

Why did I attempt suicide? By general standards, I was living the high life. I was adored, respected, and loved. I loved a man with all my heart, and he loved me as much. I had money. I wasn't technically considered rich yet, but I was getting there.

I had a legacy in sports. I had earned recognition. Most important, I was healthy and very, very happy. I shouldn't have been suicidal, but I was.

Heyday

Just six years before, I had been a newly working adult enjoying the fruits of my labor. I was the up-and-coming new agent at AIA insurance. My brand new red Toyota Corolla spoke volumes of my achievements. Or so I thought. I bought it within my first year of selling insurance, and I was determined to go for the prestigious company award—Million Dollar Round Table.

The promise of recognition called out to me, and I listened, just as I had before I took this job, when I was in school. I worked extremely hard. I pushed my body to its limits, and even though I was tired at times, I didn't heed its call to rest. History had shown me that if I put in lots of hard work and effort, I would be rewarded. History never failed people, I thought, and so it would make me proud this time, too.

History. That was the only period in my life that was full of awards, applause, and achievements. I held my head high as the entire school witnessed my name being imprinted on a plaque under the title "Sports Woman of the Year 1982." I had beaten hundreds of athletes in my secondary school to win this top honor. Not bad for a kid who grew up living in the kampong, without any riches to her name.

I had gotten all this not through luck, but through sheer hard work. When I received the award at school, my heart was beating so fast from the exhilaration that I thought it would stop on the spot. Of course, that didn't happen. Yet.

After secondary school, I was admitted into the best junior college in Singapore—Hwa Chong Junior College. At the same time, being one of the selected few who had a chance to join the national team, I was training unusually hard on my fitness and badminton. The national team! Do you know how many athletes dream of representing and bringing honor to their country? I was at my peak state of health, and my sports career was about to take off with too many bright possibilities. I had wind beneath my wings, and I knew I could soar as high as I set my sights. The world was watching me.

God speaks to us in many ways. If we don't pay attention, we might just let that all-important message slip through without knowing it. I guess God must have spoken to me when I lost my first badminton competition in front of the whole school congregation. I was a great disappointment to myself and to all who had placed their hopes and expectations in me to bring the coveted trophy home.

If I were to guess His words correctly now, He could be telling me that falls can be hard and painful, but life can still be beautiful. I can still be strong. But before I can taste the beauty of life, I need to first get up from the fall and continue walking.

It is easy to hear Him now, especially in hindsight, because I have made the choice to pay heed to His will and to live His way. But it was far from easy when He handed me the ultimate test, a lesson He meant for me to learn fast. Again, I sorely disappointed God and my loved ones. I took too long to grasp the message.

The normal route to enter university in Singapore is six years of primary school, four years of secondary school, and two years to finish junior college. The GCE "A" level results then determine if the student has a spot in the local university or not. That is a total of twelve years, the same amount of time I took to learn my lesson and get up from my next fall. Twelve long years. The average university student would have gotten his bachelor's degree, worked for two years, and maybe gone back to school to get his master's or even a doctorate. During this time when the world was moving rapidly, when China and India had begun to prosper and were fast becoming the biggest giants in Asia Pacific, when technology was advancing at a supersonic rate and economies had gone through two cycles, I remained stagnant.

The only thing I was constantly doing was breathing, and even that stopped for a while.

I had always thought I was in the pink of health. How could I not be? Wouldn't it be a big joke for a star athlete to be sickly? How could I withstand those tough training sessions that tested and pushed my body to its limits if I were less than totally fit and strong?

The fact was, I was in the red. My autoimmune system wasn't working anymore. Instead of protecting me from viruses as intended, it attacked my healthy cells and tissues. My immune system was attacking my body! I had lupus, medically known as systemic lupus erythematosus (SLE).

I remember that fateful day when I got the diagnosis. When the doctor sat me down and told me about SLE, I didn't understand what he was talking about. But I knew instinctively from his tone that something bad was happening to me. I panicked.

I had an adrenaline rush that drove my blood up. I flushed. At the time, I wished it were that simple flush a girl feeling shy would exhibit. Really, I wished I blushed like that. Because I was, after all, still a girl. I was just beginning my young adulthood at twenty years old, with so many grand dreams to fulfill and lofty goals to accomplish.

I had, in fact, a rash on my face in the shape of a butterfly, the malar rash, otherwise known as butterfly rash, the most obvious sign of a lupus patient. How apt the name, I thought sourly. I was supposed to get rich and bring lots of money home so that my grandmother and mother could have a good life. I wasn't supposed to be here!

This illness can be fatal, and it can attack any parts of the body. The lupus was hyperactive in the early days of my illness, and I suffered from many and prolonged flares, periods when the lupus was active. The time in between the flares is known as the remission period. I was seldom in remission. My condition kept worsening.

I was always fighting aches and pains, predominantly in the joints, that were so hard to bear. I often had a fever because my body was in constant battle. Physically, I was a pain to look at. Emotionally, I was a pain to live with. Normally in situations like this, when a family has a member who is sick, the whole atmosphere becomes very intense. If the patient takes it well and handles the illness positively, then the burden on the family lightens. The opposite holds true for the family if the patient does not take it well.

I belonged to the latter camp. I couldn't accept that I was suffering from lupus. It was a pill too big and hard for me to swallow. I refused to swallow it, and I showed this through my actions—very miserable, naïve, and bad actions, I must admit.

I did everything I was told not to do and didn't do anything that I was told to. I smoked heavier when I was told to quit. I went out in the sun when the doctor advised me to avoid it at all costs. I didn't take my medication on time or at all when I was, naturally, supposed to take it to keep my condition in check.

I had always had a rebellious streak in me, except that I had put it to good use when I was competing. In this case, I was vindictive. I felt bitter all the time, and indignant. I manifested all my emotions outwardly. No one in my family was allowed to laugh. Everyone had to feel as miserable as I did. Gloom hung thick at home. I vented my frustration and anger whenever I felt like it. At that time, I thought nobody would understand how I felt, and nobody could be as wretched as I was. I saw the world only with my own eyes. I had only one perspective, and that was that I didn't deserve this. I was so healthy. I worked so hard. I was so successful. This was a grave mistake.

My willfulness had consequences. Some of the consequences I had to bear myself, but most I forced my family to bear with me. Due to my exposure to the sun, I developed a skin condition called scabies. Scabies is a transmissible skin infection caused by parasites burrowing into one's skin and multiplying underneath. It produces intense, itchy skin rashes. Due to its highly infectious nature, everyone in my household had to bathe with a special liquid that smelled very bad. It was unfair to them, I knew even then, but that didn't stop me from behaving as if the whole world owed me a big favor and it was time to repay.

If life was going to treat me like this, then I didn't want any part of it anymore.

The first time I stopped breathing took me completely by surprise. When the whole episode ended, it dawned on me that this could have taken my life away when my attempted suicide had failed to do so. In the wee hours of the morning on March 17, 1994, I jolted out of sleep, grabbing my chest. I was panting and gasping for air. *What is happening to me? Why I can't breathe?* The noise woke my grandmother, who ran out to get help. My mother made two phone calls immediately, one for an ambulance and one to a neighbor.

My burly neighbor arrived first and was shocked to see me in such a state. I was wriggling on the floor, and sweat was running down my face. I had paled to a white sheet as I mustered up whatever strength I had just to take in one more pocket of oxygen. I needed oxygen desperately. Or I would die.

Isn't it funny that I had actually planned to take my own life two years earlier when I was still breathing well and happy? Now that my oxygen supply was threatening to be cut off permanently, and I could just jump into this small opportunity for death, I chickened out.

At that moment, my natural survival instinct had taken over and made the choice for me. I said I would regret twice making the choice to live, didn't I? This was the second time.

I blacked out when I was in the ambulance on my way to the hospital. When I woke up again to life, I had an extra burden to carry.

Rather than being ecstatic about my "rebirth," I lamented, "Why did you all save me? Why? Why didn't you let me die? I don't want to live anymore. Why?"

I didn't know yet that I had one more reason not to live.

A Needling Period

Have you ever seen someone carrying a huge swirling tube inserted in their neck wherever they go? Do you know how uncomfortable and bumpy the ride is? Of course, nobody would want to go through such suffering. I had no other choice because I didn't choose to die that night. I chose to breathe, and this was the price I had to pay.

The tube, known as the central venous catheter (CVC), which was connected to a dialysis machine, was to help cleanse my blood manually, given that my kidneys had failed to function completely. Patients with SLE develop many complications, and one of them is kidney failure. My breathless episode was induced by my lung being too full of water because my kidney had failed to pump it out.

Hours after I was resuscitated, my journey as a kidney patient officially commenced. The following nine years of kidney dialysis would be a grueling ordeal for my family and me, especially my grandmother. My lifestyle took a drastic turn.

The CVC is always a stop-gap measure for doctors to search for a longer-term solution, as I learned later on, because of the high risk of infection due to its location. Very soon, I was put on continual ambulatory peritoneal dialysis (CAPD). There would be two liters of dialysis fluid in my abdominal cavity, and the cleansing would take place through the natural semipermeable membrane surrounding my intestine.

I had to do this four times a day. I felt nauseated and bloated all the time. This made me feel weak, and I found the process very troublesome. I had to remember the timings of all four CAPDs and be at home getting into position whenever my alarm rang. Life seemed to revolve around that bag of fluid in my tummy, in getting it out and putting in a fresh one. It felt awkward and cumbersome to have the tube protruding from my stomach. I wished for it to end.

My prayer was answered. I endured this for a year, and then I had a fungus infection. Thus ended my days of CAPD, and I migrated to hemodialysis. I hadn't wished for this, though. Neither did I wish to get married. But I did, to a man I hardly knew but who loved me with all his heart. He was my neighbor's friend, and he frequently hung around the estate I was living in. From what I could remember, we had only made small talk. My illness didn't deter him from making his advances. When he proposed, I got the shock of my life.

"But I don't love you," I said.

"It's OK," he replied. "Feelings can be developed."

Call it a need for reliance, or security, but what he said moved me so much that I said yes.

We registered our marriage four months after I was diagnosed with kidney failure. As the saying goes, "Every cloud has a silver lining." This was my first peek at brightness since gloom had taken over me.

Whether it was for better or worse, I didn't know. I mean the hemodialysis.

Hemodialysis requires an access point, known as the fistula, to connect a Y-shaped catheter tube from the machine to the blood vessels. The fistula was usually constructed at the forearm, but my too-small veins prevented this. What was I to expect? I wasn't "normal," right? Therefore, we opted for the next best solution—the vascular graft. The location selected was my left upper arm.

The graft was a tube about 12 inches long and 6 millimeters in diameter. Just imagine a tube the size of a ballpoint pen with a little swirl implanted right under the skin. In the next four years of using this graft, I had three operations to clear away blood clots in the tube. As a lupus patient, I was tested as "lupus anticoagulant positive." That means my blood clots much faster than that of the normal person. Oral blood thinner medications were added to my daily burden of doses. More blood thinner had to be injected into the tube whenever I was doing dialysis too.

The graft eventually deteriorated to a condition that couldn't be salvaged anymore. It had to be removed. A major surgery ensued because tissues had grown over the graft and had to be carefully separated before the tube was removed.

The second graft was in my right upper arm. The last one was in my right thigh, close to the groin area. Not the best location, but I had to make do with it. I was in agony, while fighting to survive other complications of lupus.

"Make do with it" and "Live with it" were two mottos that slowly became my close friends.

I had to live with the pain. I had to make do with the temporary CVC in my neck so frequently that the holes barely healed before I had to prick open another. I had to live with not having a shower at all whenever the CVC was inserted in my neck, or in my chest at one point. I had to make do with all sorts of irritation and distress. I learned to live with most things that were happening to me, especially those that were beyond my control.

But I couldn't live with one fact, a fact that was grilled into me when the doctors first announced I had kidney failure.

Every kidney patient has a dream. Besides living as normal a life as possible while undergoing daily dialysis, kidney patients dream of having a successful transplant. Demand is extremely high compared with the enormously low supply. We have to wait for a suitable kidney to come up. There is nothing we can do but wait.

I wanted to wait for my chance. To be on the waiting list is the single shred of hope any kidney patient can hang on to.

Alas, my doctor mercilessly cut that off. She said, "Jacklyn, you can't be on the waiting list for kidney transplant." "Why?" I asked. Was it because I wasn't rich? Why? Why couldn't I get to wait?

"Because you have lupus. Even if you have the transplant, your immune system will attack the new organ, and at the end, the kidney will fail again. So we need to take this into consideration and weigh the benefits of you versus someone else without lupus taking that kidney."

I couldn't get a transplant? If I was hearing right, my doctor was telling me I would have to be on dialysis for as long as I live. I couldn't accept this! I didn't want to live with this fact. Not this. No matter how adamant I was, my name was struck from the waiting list. It was like the biggest, tightest slap in the face I ever experienced.

How could I survive this? How could I still find a meaning to live on? How could anyone find a meaning to live on?

The Reasons to Live

I believe that God occasionally sends angels to us in times of hardship, when we feel that we are drowning. I have had the good fortune to have several angels in my life.

My grandmother had always been my greatest source of encouragement, comfort, strength, motivation, and love. She was the one who stopped me short of jumping to my death. She pulled me back from the brink of giving up and onto the solid ground of well-being.

We were very close, possibly because she had cared for me since I was three years old, when my parents divorced. She accompanied me to all my checkups, and she seemed to be there each time I was hospitalized. I would not be who I am now if not for her. I would not have survived till now, and be living so healthily, if not for her.

She woke me up and made me realize the power of choosing.

No choices were too hard to make until I was faced with choosing an option that was neither the best nor what I wanted. But it was a choice that I had to make. It was a choice of no choice. Have you ever experienced this? Have you ever faced a situation and explored possible decisions, only to realize that no matter how many alternatives you can think of, there will be more than one reason to forbid any of those solutions? At that instant, you really feel helpless. No matter how much you want to do something, you can't. That is how powerless and vulnerable I felt.

Yet in the face of such adversity, when I was feeling defenseless, love was the antidote. It gave me the strength I needed, the perseverance I had to have, and the motivation that drove me on. Love from my grandmother, mother, husband, friends, and the source of all love, God.

The miracle happened on one afternoon when I was lying in the hospital. As usual, my grandmother was sitting beside me. It would have been another ordinary day if not for the epiphany I had. I finally woke up, and at that point, the decision I chose to make really made all the difference in my life. At last, I crossed the threshold. I was no longer a victim of circumstances. I would fight on. I would survive.

The choice to take full responsibility for my life, especially my health, turned my condition around. I started taking my medication on time, every time. I psyched myself up to remain positive, and I looked for a job. Despite being rejected many times, and having to put up with all the strange stares of the interviewers, I found an income source with the only skill I had. I became a taxi driver. I started to provide for my living and my medical fees.

I felt very sorry for being such a burden to my family, who had to resort to borrowing money to finance my medical bills because they were fully drained. I wanted to make it up.

When a friend called me sometime in 1998 to introduce me to a health supplement, I was unwilling to hear her out. Any health supplement that you could name, I'd probably taken it already. But she persisted for five months, and finally I relented. I agreed to attend a talk by the founder of the company, Dr. Jau-Fei Chen, a scientist who had won several prestigious awards.

I was so impressed with the technology and science behind the whole concept of nutritional immunology Dr. Chen presented that I became a consumer right away. I didn't know what was going to happen to me. I just knew that there was no harm taking the supplements because they were just wholesome foods to boost the immune system. I needed that, didn't I?

Remember the year—it was 1999.

The first few months after I started taking the products, my blood test results were erratic. My doctor was very concerned and asked me if I was taking health supplements again. I said yes, and I told her I was eating products from E. Excel. She advised me to stop taking them, but I told her I was feeling good. In fact, as much as my reports showed otherwise, I was feeling, for the first time, healthy! I felt fit, and I could sense this surge of energy welling up inside me. It was a very strange sensation, something that I couldn't explain but totally relished. So I decided to continue taking the products.

It must have been God's arrangement. Maybe my positive frame of mind helped, too. By September 1999, the lupus index dropped to a near normal level. The index is an indicator of the lupus activity level. The decreasing number merely translated to this jaw-dropping, near-heavenly piece of good news for me and my family—my lupus was in remission!

How could this happen? I didn't know. All I knew was this was the best thing that had happened to me since I'd been diagnosed thirteen years ago. I thought my ears were playing a trick on me, but I quickly reconfirmed the fact—remission. I was ecstatic.

My faith in Dr. Chen and the products grew so strong that I lunged into promoting nutritional immunology as my full-time career. My business as a distributor grew in leaps and bounds. In a record-breaking time of merely three years, I was promoted to the level of Jade Ambassador in E. Excel in November 2001. That was the biggest achievement in my life, and so much more treasured because it hadn't come easy at all. The journey I took from suffering from the biggest setback in my life to overcoming all the anger and self-denial and finally summoning up my willpower to fight this battle was a long one. The tears I shed, the pain I endured, were all worth it after all. Most important, I could face my late grandmother and tell her I had done it. I hadn't given up. When she was still alive, she had always taught me never to give up.

Glad tidings follow each other. I believe that good energy begets good energy. While all of us were jumping for joy, I received news. I rewrote history. I defied what the doctors thought was impossible, took the impossible and made it possible. I was, after all, eligible to have a kidney transplant. I had created a miracle.

In a transplant, there is a donor and a recipient. I was the recipient, and the honor of the donor was taken by none other than my mom. For once, I wanted to go under the knife as soon as possible. But before I could do that, we needed to do something about her health, because she had failed the donor's test. The kidney was suitable, fortunately. Her state of health, however, wasn't satisfactory for an operation. Without further ado, I put her on E. Excel's products. She was cleared in the end. I was one step closer to making my dream come true. I could smell it already. I was that close. The date was set: February 20, 2002.

I was in the operating theater sooner, on February 2, 2002. But not for the kidney transplant.

The most unexpected event happened—again. Life is full of ups and downs, but I guess mine hardly consisted of any plateaus. I stopped breathing again, almost. I suffered my first heart attack. When I was rushed to the hospital, I was informed that I had to go through an angioplasty procedure to clear the blocked arteries caused by my blood clots.

I had a flashback on my journey, of all the things that I hadn't done yet and what I needed to do. I was so scared that I wouldn't wake up from this surgery. I knew I would hang on to every living opportunity, and my willpower was too strong to allow me to leave with so many unfulfilled wishes. Not even the excruciating pain (I wasn't on general anesthesia) I had to tolerate during the procedure could dampen my spirits. I knew my mom was waiting for me outside. She must have been very anxious. I had to hang on for her sake.

My arteries were cleared, and my heart pumped normally again. But when something is done to an organ, we can't expect it to regain its pre-operation state. The risk of another heart attack was very real. For this reason, my transplant was called off again. Doctors declared that now I was unfit for a transplant because it would pose a big risk to my heart.

I didn't put up any fight with them this time. The heart attack had suddenly made me realize that life can be fragile. No matter how hard I worked to be healthy, how much I wanted to have a better quality of life by taking responsibility and positive actions, I could easily die of a heart attack. This is life. Since I couldn't beat it, then why bother continuing? I gave up again.

I returned to a despondent state. I didn't believe in myself anymore, and I no longer believed I was in control of my health. Sensing that I probably was going to give up, God brought another angel to my side.

His name is Kelvyn, and he is my mentor in E. Excel. I respect him a lot, and he deserves every bit of my high opinion. Kelvyn is a Malaysian who came to Singapore, and he knew that I had chosen to give up and not continue this battle anymore. He said something to me that shook me up and changed my perspective in that instant.

"Jacklyn, since you decided to fight back, you've created miracles."

Tears rolled down my cheeks. I was so touched. I couldn't speak for the next five minutes as I sobbed in front of him. What had I to say? Kelvyn was right. I had created miracles! By believing in myself, in God, and in hope, I had created miracles. Who says a lupus patient cannot have kidney transplant?

I crossed the second threshold once more, and I became a stronger fighter. After my operation, I doubled my dosage of the products, and I walked until I was exhausted daily to exercise my body. I had to build up my health. I needed to be strong.

My body bounced back. Doctors, who had announced that I was unfit for the transplant operation, had to take back their words again. Results showed that I was fit. I won the battle again. I triumphed. Now came the real test.

The new date was set—October 9, 2002.

On the eve of this day, my faith was put to the test again. My doctor came to visit me and ran down a list of all the risks I had to face during the operation. My chance of a successful operation was only 50 percent, giving me almost enough reasons to forget about the procedure. At that time, I had only one thing on my mind, and that was to get out of this dialysis trap and to focus on a good quality of living. I knew God would give me His blessings, because He had given me a peace that I hadn't felt so strongly before.

With this peace, on October 9, I woke up in the intensive care unit in Singapore General Hospital. I knew my surgery had been successful, and I felt so relieved. I had finally dumped the heavy weight I had carried for years. A deep feeling of peace and calm swept through me and stayed with me throughout my days in the ICU and the high dependency unit, where I spent time recuperating with no one else but God.

My recovery wasn't without any hiccups, though. A complication developed in my liver, and I grew worried. But my faith stood by me, and I emerged from this episode fairly unharmed. I praised the Lord for His blessings, and I was most grateful.

Learning to be grateful for even the smallest things in life that we tend to take for granted has been very useful for me. If I used to take the results of every action seriously, I have now learned to cherish the process even more. I learned the greatness of forgiveness.

I felt bad that my mother had to go through an operation at her age, so the best way to repay her was to live my life to the fullest.

I brought her along on my trips whenever I traveled. We are now much closer to each other than when I was still a kid.

I have gone through so much and come to this point in my life now that I want to say this—life does have miracles. Sometimes we create them from the choices we make. Sometimes they are given to us from the choices others make. And now, I like to think that maybe, SLE is my miracle. Without it, I wouldn't have seen the world in so many different lights. I wouldn't have such a story to share, and I wouldn't be who I am today.

I have a brand new attitude toward life and living. I guess after all these ups and downs, the one thing that remains unchanged is my view toward love. Love is the common denominator where all my motivation lies.

With love, we can create miracles, when we begin to realize we have the power of choice.

About the Author

Jacklyn Ker manages a thriving trade as the independent distributor of E. Excel International, a U.S.-based nutritional immunology products company. She was awarded the highly respected title of Jade Ambassador three years into the business as a result of her stellar performance and positive attitude. She often speaks at major company events and conventions to motivate and inspire fellow distributors.

Jacklyn is the author of *When Life Lights Your Darkest Hour*. She blogs on inspiration and empowerment at www.JacklynKer.com and is also a licensed master practitioner of Neuro-Linguistics Programming with the Society of NLP (USA).

She is a life coach for individuals who are facing challenges in life. A strong believer in personal development, Jacklyn uses her skills in NLP to assist these people in making breakthroughs in their lives and achieving goals. She currently lives in Singapore with her mother and two pet dogs.

Never Give Up on Your Dreams

Kissmea Naude

I am from a black working-class family and was reared most of my life in a township called Bonteheuwel on the Cape Flats, South Africa, a place rife with gangsterism and drug use, where killing was an everyday happening. I always knew that I wanted to be different. I always knew that I wanted to be the boss. My parents could not afford to keep me at school so I left school with a matric certificate (high school). In those years of apartheid, things were difficult. We were suppressed as a people, and I fell in love with a white boy who came from the country areas of George, from a very anti-black white family. At the age of nineteen I got pregnant, and I thought my whole world would collapse because I would now be arrested for getting pregnant by a white boy. Little did I know that my world would not collapse but would eventually grow beyond my wildest dreams.

Realizing My Goals

I had always excelled in my career before I became a businesswoman, but I lasted no longer than a year in any job; after that, I became bored with the repetition of my administrative duties. There had to be more. When I diversified into sales and became very successful, I knew I had found my calling. I became number one in the world with an international cookware company and won a trip to Switzerland, realizing my dreams of traveling. Then disaster struck, and I was fired from my position as sales manager. I lost everything: my car, house, husband—everything.

Personal development was my vice (and my virtue). I read and studied anything and everything that would add value to me as an individual. I followed the advice of people like Brian Tracy, Zig Ziglar, and so on. This gave me the power and knowledge to do what the professionals do in whatever subject I wanted to study. I finished my degrees part time and started studying for an MBA with the Business School of Netherlands. In 1995, after I was fired from my sales manager position, I started marketing a pesticide from my flat, using students to go door to door to sell the product. I had three small children to look after whose father did not support us in any way whatsoever. Business grew so quickly that I opened offices in the center of Cape Town, and when my clients requested that I provide them with pest control services, I added it as a new division. Business grew from strength to strength, even though I had many obstacles in the way. I bought a car first because I'd had to borrow family's and friends' cars to go and see my clients.

Obstacles

I experienced many obstacles, like race—I was not white enough for the corporate world of South Africa, and businesses did not want to take chances. But I did not give up, and with the help of some white individuals with good hearts, who agreed to give a black business a chance, I started closing big contracts with corporate clients.

Being a black woman in business also presented problems. I started with 20 cents in my pocket. No financing at all. Banks were not really interested in lending money to a black woman with no business expertise. I had to win the trust of my suppliers to receive short-term credit. I lived hand to mouth for half of my business career.

Believe in Yourself

I was positive amid all the negativity of business and believed in myself. I was not going to fail at any cost. I had to make this a success because I now had the taste of my lifelong dream to be the boss and make my own decisions.

Doors were constantly slammed in my face, but I was consistent and determined that I would make this a success. During the day, I was out on the road marketing my business. After hours, I was doing most of the administrative work as well as getting my systems in place to run a successful business. I burned the midnight oil, sending faxes at two o'clock in the morning. My friends thought I was crazy. I had no social life, but I knew the sacrifices I made would benefit me in the long run. In 1997 I started another company, which I made successful in the first year in a male-dominated industry: security. I traveled to London on a sponsorship of the British Council and studied the CCTV street systems and other related services in the security industry and visited a trade show relevant to the industry in London. This became an annual event, and I was one of the first South African companies to conclude a partnership with the British security industry, bringing world-class training in that industry to South Africa.

Furthering My Goals

I was nominated to the first South African standard-generating body to set standards in the industry and was the first woman on this board. Because of my excellent networking, I was exposed to government and corporate leaders in the industry and launched one of the biggest women's investment groups in the western cape. I was appointed to the committee of a large investment group to deal with the apportionment of funds donated to women's charities. I was also appointed as the vice chairperson of one of the biggest business chambers in the western cape, heading up the opportunities section. With one of the first and biggest casinos in the western cape opening, I was selected as the small business partner with a big corporation, and I secured all the service-related contracts for this casino. This was my biggest accomplishment ever.

Obstacles struck again when I was divorced in 1999. This was a great setback because I'd thought I had met my life partner. I suffered depression and lost a lot of money during this time because my attention was not fully on my business. A year later I took control of the situation. I ploughed myself into my business, and it took me two years to take it further and grow 400 percent in turnover. I then added two new companies to the portfolio, which are now in a growth phase. During all this time I had to put my children through school, but I could offer them employment in the family business. Today my son, at the age of twenty-nine, has been newly appointed to take over the operational reins of my group of three companies. I know now that despite everything, I will leave a legacy.

About the Author

Kissmea Naude resides in the Cape Town area in South Africa and is the owner of her own company, Bluedot Facilities. She is an inspiration to everyone she meets.

My Gift to You

Waheeda Aziz

Imagine how you would feel if everyone around you had limited belief that you would make it through. Imagine that your presence for some is a heavy burden, and for others, joy and happiness.

Imagine that your frequent visits to the hospital due to your health challenges become a normal part of everyone's world, and as time goes on, your friends and family don't worry anymore.

Imagine being in chronic pain that disturbs your breathing, blurs your vision, and dulls your hearing so that you hear nothing except your heartbeat, like a loaded drum with a gradually slowing pace.

Now imagine a tiny ball inside you that glows so bright, that gives you a warm feeling from deep within yourself, showing you hope and giving you the courage to fight all the tears, pain, and medical expectations.

All that you have imagined is my reality.

I live my life by giving and receiving love from my family and from all the beings that cross my path. We all have our own interpretations and definitions of love. However, my definition of love is a way of life. Love is the air I breathe to go on. It's hope that brings me solutions to challenges. It's the castle that shelters my world, and it's the inspirational engine that drives my dreams.

Only when everyone saw me die did I realize that I can walk, run, jump, and fly off the ground—gravity can't hold me down. I never put any limits to my imagination of who I can become and how I define my life's purpose. When closing my eyes, I picture a silent sea of green, and my vision goes as far as where the sky meets the sea. I use this image as an outline for my life, and even though tomorrow is not promised, I live with great belief that I will achieve all that I am here for.

Born in London, I was raised, with three brothers, to believe that conventional education is everything. People will respect you if you have a degree, and you will get a good job and live a happy life. Even though my parents do not have conventional degrees, they expected us to earn them. My father is a self-made successful businessman. He came to London before marrying my mother and lived in a shared house while working as a waiter. He is the eldest child and cared not only for himself but also for his siblings and my grandparents. He had a dream of owning a restaurant to provide him enough finances to help with his responsibilities. My father was inspired and motivated by his dream so much that his eagerness helped him learn the trade very quickly, and he was soon promoted to manager of the Indian restaurant where he worked. He went back to Bangladesh because his parents wished for him to bring a bride into the house, and he married my mother. Five years passed before my parents were able to join each other in London and start their family. My mother did not have enough qualifications to work outside the home, and because we were babies and we had a disabled brother, she dedicated all of her time to us. With her hands full of responsibilities, she still wanted to help my father reach his dreams. Mum had a hobby of tailoring clothing, and she decided to work from home part time making dresses for clothing shops. Through my mother's part-time work and my father's work in different restaurants, as well as mixing with the people who were already living his dreams, my parents saved between them enough capital to open their own restaurant. This began spinning the wheel of success for them. The principles my father used to achieve this success were not taught in schools, colleges, and universities. I always used to wonder how he took on such a huge responsibility and what gave him the courage. Becoming successful like my father was added to my wish list.

As I was growing up, I saw my parents struggle with one of my brothers, who was born physically and mentally disabled. I was born premature at four pounds and was very underdeveloped, which made me receptive to illnesses. I never realized that I also required attention. I was always assisting my parents with my brothers. Everyone knew they could rely on me because I would always put others first and never worry about myself. I taught our youngest brother, who is three years younger than I am, to walk, and even to this day he says he learned how to walk by holding on to his sister's little finger and therefore knows he is blessed to walk through life.

From a very young age I enjoyed writing my feelings into rhymes and making them into creative stories and poems. I would make the writing fun to read and seal it with a smile. I was too shy to share it with my friends and used to release some of my material in the college internal magazine. Even then I would never sign it with my real name. This internal magazine used to be released every month, and I would always be excited to hear my friends' opinions of the writing. I never shared this talent with my parents because they had different expectations of me. They wanted me to be a doctor. And just to please them, I decided to take an interest in that field. So many of us do not know what career we would like to have, and therefore we decide to live someone else's expectation. What is even more of a shame is that even if we realize we are not passionate about the field we've chosen, we are often too afraid to change paths. We just carry on living a life for someone else, and our dreams are just paintings, nice to look at but not truly real.

That was exactly what I was doing. I made myself think that I was passionate about it, and even though some topics seemed interesting, I did not understand many other topics and had no motivation to find out about them. That was obviously the first sign for me, but I decided to brush it under the carpet and just carry on living my parents' expectations, hoping that I would make them proud. But I didn't get the grades I needed to get into medical school, and the disappointment in my parents' eyes made me feel like a failure. At the time I wrote the following, and I share it here for the first time.

The world seems intensely selfish today.
So self-centered they live each day.
I never thought the people who love me so much could turn their back.
Not sure where to hide my face; I was convinced that I majorly lacked.
So much betrayal and unseen deceit,
Within split seconds I was hurt and became concrete.
But how come I never noticed this before?
Gave so much love and was waiting to receive more.
I've never been here; I feel so trapped; I'm searching for another door.
I conclude today that I will always come back to the same old feeling.
I believe I will get out of it; it's just a different type of healing.

I was lost for a while and not sure what to do with my life. I started experimenting with things in my head. I would visualize situations, almost see them in front of me like premonitions, and I realized that I was attracting these kinds of situations in my life. The process was vey intense. I put great thought and feelings into what I would visualize. My first experiments were to do with my health challenges. I was severely anemic and had to take pills and other medicines for a very long time. I had poor blood circulation, and the doctors told me that I would need a bone marrow transplant. I have a universal blood type, which means that I can give to others but cannot easily receive; therefore transplants were also a difficult matter because my body would reject any new marrow and cause more problems, which would be hard to reverse. I strongly believe that illnesses can be cured through an individual's belief system and mindset, and I hated the thought of inserting manmade medication into my body.

I loved physical activities, such as playing netball and badminton, but as I got older, I tired very quickly and couldn't finish games. I was very disappointed when I was selected to play for the home boroughs' team but could not physically sustain the game. I would feel faint and dizzy doing normal things like walking or bike riding. My activities were limited. I could not accept this, being separated from everyday normal things. We never separated my disabled brother from doing activities and receiving schooling because we did not want him to feel different in any way. Even when my brothers and I lived away from home, going to school and exploring and learning how to live independent lives, we found a special needs college for our disabled brother so that he would experience the same. I was adamant about listening to my heart and knowing that I would get through this, and by visualizing and working on my mindset, I have become a living miracle who has made it through on the strength of thought. I accept that medical experts are highly trained and base their opinions on highly researched facts, and I totally respect that, but there is something that is much richer than that—self-belief.

I have read about people who have cured themselves, and I strongly believe in that. If there is something that you want from the deepest compartment of your heart, there are no limits to it. You can achieve everything and anything you desire. Your destiny is your choice.

The sweetest and most intimate secret I have learned about life started from seeing my father meet his dreams with the help of my mother through their life's struggles. I applied the same principles and am living my life's purpose. Every second counts, and I allow myself to live life to its full potential. I dearly enjoy my time, whether it is with family and friends or when making a positive difference, even just putting a smile on a stranger's face.

So just stop everything you are doing, take a step back, and silently indulge in yourself for a few minutes a day. Ask yourself if you are happy with what you are becoming through what you are doing. If you are not, then have the courage to take two steps back and one desirable step forward. Life is about living with unconditional love and making your dreams come true. Live with your dreams, not without them.

In conclusion I share with you what I have found out about my purpose:

This is ME
My life, my belief, is God's gift to me.
What I do with it is my gift to God.

The one thing that can never let you down is yourself.
Belief, trust, and love all have meanings which only you can make concise.
The definitions of these are what you conquer and produce for yourself
Don't allow what the eye can see hypnotize you.

I give you my love unconditionally.
It's dangerous only if you take advantage horribly.
My dream is to leave behind footprints in the form of a legacy.
My path in this journey can only be sustainability.

There is light at the end of this tunnel. and my vision is now clear
I do not just see the primary colors of this rainbow. which was so dear.
The tertiary colors are now apparent, all is so near.
I will challenge all hurdles with no fear.

Once upon a time it was cloudy; a little light had a strong beam.
I captured the smallest sparkle and manifested this gleam.
Every success has hurdles and defeats. but it's not as hard as it seems.
For now I have an inspiring team to transpire my awakening dream.

My life, my belief, is God's gift to me.
What I do with it is my gift to God.

About the Author

Waheeda Aziz lives in London, where she uses her passion for inspiring others to make a positive difference in the lives of everyone she comes in contact with.

Attitude of Gratitude

Paul P. Clarke

When I was invited to share a chapter in this enriching follow-up to the first volume of *Multiple Streams of Inspiration*, I was truly grateful. To join other international names, people who have overcome different adversities in their lives and established themselves as success stories, was an honor for an entrepreneur from a small island in the Caribbean. It really just goes to show you, it's not about the size of your island but more about the size of your story. I saw this as the perfect opportunity to share some of the principles from my upcoming book *The Jesus Element*, principles that propelled me from being one hundred thousand dollars in debt to financial independence in less than one year. In preparing my chapter, my initial plan was to discuss a couple of the principles that worked for me and create a mini-stampede toward my other book.

That plan soon changed. After recently having to provide frequent explanations of some questionable circumstances in my life a couple years ago, I decided to take this opportunity to offer some very public answers.

Life Lessons

It is truly amazing the unconditional love that you see in the eyes of a child. The amazement becomes unexplainably magnified when that child is your own. I can still clearly remember the first day I locked eyes with each of my children. Daily, meeting eyes with them is filled with the joy of seeing them for the first time all over again. Your children always seem so excited to see you, as if you were more to them than their favorite nursery rhyme or a brand new shiny toy, as if they know that you are living your entire life for them and through their eyes. That pure feeling that pours through their eyes is what I usually describe as an attitude of gratitude. It was that attitude, that principle, which brought me through the most tumultuous time in my life.

In December 2005 I learned my biggest business lesson—the hard way. I had a business partner whose only business input was his time. (Note to self: If a person is only putting in his time and not capital investment, do *not* make him an equal business partner.) The business relationship ended due to different points of view, and not amicably. In fact, he signed and received $65,000 on my behalf, and that was just the beginning. He then proceeded to slander my name with anyone who would listen, which began to put a strain on many of my business and personal relationships, but I thought eventually he would realize his miscalculations and walk away. I have never been so wrong.

During all this, I was spending more time exploring the personal development industry. I met Johnny Wimbrey for the first time, in January 2006, as he was introducing a group of people to a new opportunity at the Hilton in Barbados. Most people there saw it as a business opportunity, but the lucky ones saw it for what it truly was—a life opportunity. Halfway through his presentation, explaining his own life story, Johnny took out a hundred-dollar bill and asked the audience, "Who wants this hundred?" All hands present filled the air, and then Johnny did something that helped construct one of the most memorable personally defining moments in my life. He crumpled the bill in his hand, dropped it on the floor, stomped on it, and then asked the confused crowd, "Who wants it now?" All of the same hands went in the air, and then Johnny explained the purpose of the exercise. The hundred-dollar bill still had the same worth despite being crumpled and stomped on, much like all of us in our lives at some point. Then he said, "Never let anyone's opinion of you become your reality." As he repeated it, I knew it was powerful, but I didn't realize that this one statement would be a driving force in my life.

Around March 2006, I was picking myself up and getting life together after those major financial losses. My wife and I had a core business in event and media management, which was supplemented by some newfound life principles and revenue from Success University, the personal development website. Never short on ideas, I managed to attract some major investors for a possible multimillion dollar real estate deal, but as we were 90 percent to finalizing the deal, it all came crumbling down. On March 21, 2006, the police questioned me about previous business relations with the same business partner from my past. A couple days before that, while on a routine bank checkup, I realized that he was involved in forging my signature on a bank instrument to a local telecommunications provider. Based on the investigators' line of questioning, my lawyer and good friend advised me not to comment. The investigators took it upon themselves to conduct a search of my property and office and wrongfully charged me with forging a bank document without proper investigation or even simply following the blatant paper trail.

On searching my property, they found the documents on which he had forged my signature, and they told me I should file a counter complaint against my ex-partner. This should have been their first hint to investigate further, but instead I had to spend the night in a holding facility until they figured out what to do. That night I was at peace as I remembered the look in my son's eyes as he lay next to me the night before as well as Johnny's demonstration with the hundred-dollar bill. In my mind, I kept replaying three Success University courses, but the one that seemed most appropriate was Willie Jolly's "A Setback Is a Setup for a Comeback." No truer words have ever been said.

The next day my face was splashed in the local newspaper, "Bank Manager Charged with $80,000 Fraud." The story read as though I had stolen money from the bank I had resigned from at the end of 2003. What was funny was that I had never held the position of bank manager, but that didn't stop the public from believing the article. That same day, the real estate deal fell apart, and all the phones that had been constantly ringing with "friends" and other business associates fell silent. Other than my family and true friends, no one reached out to me in what I thought was my time of need. After spending about two days alone, crying, locked away in the house, wondering why this had happened to me, I submerged myself again in personal development material. My lawyers were ready to take legal proceedings against the police for wrongfully charging me, the newspaper for libel, and my ex-partner for forgery, but something told me to wait.

The Comeback

While I was now making little to no money in my normal businesses, I was able to support my family on the relationships I had built through Success University alone.

After being invited by Johnny Wimbrey to his Speak for Cash speaker's training in Dallas, I was able to find my voice. It was truly a life-changing experience: I was able to build new relationships with like-minded people such as my good friend Bobby Minor, the effervescent "Coke," and many others who helped me realize, as Les Brown says, "It's not over until you win."

I spent the rest of 2006 and early 2007 rebuilding, traveling, and speaking. I dedicated my time to spreading the word of overcoming adversity, speaking mostly with early grade school kids, parents, and teachers. My main topic was, "Are You a Noun or a Verb?" The purpose was to motivate the kids to be anything that they wanted to be and to encourage the parents and teachers to support those ideas.

Exactly one year to the day of my newspaper fiasco, I was again in the press, but this time I was hosting the largest festival of events on the island, and that was just the beginning. From there, in April 2007, my wife and I embarked on two completely new business ventures, again with the faith and assistance of some family members and investors. We took on projects completely different from anything we had ever done before, but because of the business and life experiences we had recently encountered, we knew we would excel. All of the people who had stopped calling suddenly remembered the digits, but we now knew exactly who they were.

It was a bittersweet coincidence when one of the business ideas I had been sitting on for over three years was picked up for title sponsorship by the same telecommunications company where my ex-business partner was now working. By the way, this is the same company involved in manipulating my signature on a bank instrument. I knew that if I saw him now, I would be more inclined to tell him thank you for his participation in my journey.

I had to supply these answers for two reasons. First, I hope others can learn from my experience, and second, I really got tired of responding to people one on one about the situation. I need to move on, and I have no intention of taking legal action against my ex-partner, the police, or the newspaper—at this time.

I am just thankful for all of these circumstances because they led me to realize who I am and Whose I am. Thanks, Johnny! I am now at a place in my life where I am in a better position to help others. Today, I have a family that loves me and a group of successful businesses, and we are now breaking ground on our dream home, without a mortgage.

I mention my recent successes not to impress you but more to impress upon you the importance of cultivating and maintaining an attitude of gratitude. You must be thankful and grateful for what you currently have, because it is only then that more of life's treasures will be bestowed on you. Your attitude is the first step on the journey to discovering who you are, which is essential in unleashing in you what I have termed "The Jesus Element." I sincerely encourage you to read this entire book cover to cover and allow my friends to help inspire you to move forward in a positive way in your life. I will leave you with this thought, originally credited to Winston Churchill: "Attitudes are contagious. Are yours worth catching?"

About the Author

With numerous titles—successful entrepreneur, life coach, marketing executive, and author—Paul Clarke is most proud of his role as a husband and a father. Living in the Caribbean island of Barbados, his quest for purpose began in December 2004, after the passing of his grandfather, who helped mold him into the family man he is today. His thirst for truth on his journey led him to the path of personal development and to working with great names such as Les Brown, Matt Morris, and Johnny Wimbrey, to name a few. Paul's amazing and inspiring story of overcoming personal and financial adversity has been captured in his new book, *The Jesus Element*, where he explores basic life principles necessary for success in any aspect of one's life. The principles he freely shares have helped him recover and excel through difficult circumstances and have made it possible for him to create a legacy for his children's children.

An Open Mind with a Vision

Stephen Metcalfe

This is a story about air travel, something many people do routinely yet few truly appreciate for its quiet potential to enhance our lives in small ways. We're focused on the destination and often bored and irritated during the journey, wishing the time away and therefore wishing our lives away. But it doesn't have to be that way.

For two years, I've been planning a trip to the United States to attend the Main Event by the Di Lemme Development Group. I wasn't able to attend in March 2007 because I was working offshore; however, everything seemed to fall into place for me in 2008. Not only was I free of work obligations, but as soon as I heard that the infamous Coach Carter was again contributing his time to be there, I wrote down in my notebook, "I will be attending the Main Event in March 2008." I wrote that statement in April 2007, and I reread it a few times each week with a passionate hope that it would come true.

Today was the day I drove myself to the airport. My two younger daughters, Jessica and Sharlene, came along for the ride but would be returning home with the car as soon as I reached the airport. As usual, I left as late as possible, because I had many things to attend to before yet another five- to six-week trip overseas. On my return from the Main Event in Atlanta, Georgia, I planned to stop in Thailand to catch up with old work friends and associates I had met in the mid-1990s.

After stopping at the Perth Airport departure terminal, I hugged Jessica and kissed her goodbye. I told Sharlene I was sorry I wouldn't be home for her tenth birthday, but I said I would buy her something special from the Internet and have it delivered. I always like to leave some type of anticipation and excitement in my daughters' lives, however small it may be. I think it's important they know that, while I am overseas, I am thinking of them all the time.

As I waved goodbye to my daughters, I turned toward the airport terminal somewhat relieved to see that, in my rush, I had made it to the airport with just under two hours before departure; this would give me enough time to check in and look around. However, when I entered the terminal, I was somewhat surprised to see what must have been the longest line of people I'd ever seen, also waiting to check in. Close to two hundred people were in line, and I quickly joined the growing queue.

While waiting, I realized I had a perfect opportunity to listen to an interview I had previously purchased and downloaded onto my MP3 player. This would be a great use of my time spent in line because I'd get my mind thinking about tasks and priorities I had previously set for myself. I didn't want to be lured into the boredom I saw on the faces of most other people waiting. I always look for opportunities outside the norm, or pockets of time during the day when I can achieve more than one objective at the same time.

I think it was Jim Rohn who said something like, "The wind blows on all of us, but it is the set of the sails, not the direction of the wind, that determines which way we will go." Another of my favorite quotes is from Les Browne: "It's not what happens to us that counts, for what happens to us, happens to everyone. It's what we do with it that makes the difference." To me, these two statements stress the importance of a positive outlook, and they form the basis of how I greet each day. I am further guided by three powerful quotes from John Di Lemme:

"What you do today, predicts your future."
"What you do behind the scenes changes the scenery."
"If you don't own your future, someone else will."

After an hour wait that seemed short, I was checked in, had passed immigration, and was on my way to board my flight. As the aircraft proceeded down the runway, I was able to reflect on the somewhat good lifestyle I had created for myself.

Shortly after leaving high school, with a brief taste of the everyday working life, I could never visualize myself settling into the nine-to-five shuffle. I thought that surely there must be more to life than this. Why, I wondered, would any man kiss his wife in the morning and go his way, off to work, while she went her way for the better part of the day? Then husband and wife return home at night, only to go through a ritual that seems to prepare them for more of the same the following day.

That's not living. How could it possibly be?

So after six months of going through this routine, minus the wife, I decided to opt out and return to university studies. At least this would give me hope for a better future. But I didn't just delay my return to the rat race. I did much better than that. I enrolled in a course of study that would open up international doors.

I'm a geophysicist, and I have been working offshore on research vessels for the past fifteen years. This role has taken me all over the world. I've been to Tasmania in Australia, and I've gone throughout

Southeast Asia, including the Philippines, Vietnam, Indonesia, Singapore, Malaysia, and Myanmar. I've also been to India, Africa, Brazil, Mexico, the United States, and Canada. It has been a very rewarding experience, for I have met many great people from different countries and cultures.

Praise God that one of the greatest decisions I ever made in my life, one that affects me to this very day, was my decision to live in Thailand. In April 1996 I decided to live on the island of Phuket. This is where I met my beautiful wife, Apuntee. I still can remember one of my wife's very early letters in which she had written that she dreamed of the day when she'd be married to me, living in our own house with our own beautiful children.

We eventually moved to Perth, Western Australia, happily married with our three very lovely daughters, Jessica, Sharlene, and Namfon, who are 8, 10, and 16, respectively. Unfortunately, our marriage lasted only seven years. Mysteriously, we drifted apart, and today we are separated. Separation seems to happen to most people in the offshore geophysical industry, but I'm determined not to let it sway my focus on building a lifestyle that will allow me to kiss the offshore life goodbye, become a mentor to my children, and have them sharing in my lifestyle.

The flight arrived in Bangkok on time. After collecting my luggage, I was on my way to my hotel room downtown. I hadn't been back to Thailand in four years and was only in transit, but I would soon return for a relaxing break. The next day I checked out at 1 p.m., which was six hours before my flight. From previous experience with Bangkok traffic, I felt it was better to allow plenty of time. I actually reached the Suvarnadhumi International Airport five hours before my flight. Suvarnadhumi is Bangkok's new airport, and it is enormous, with many shops and restaurants. So even though I was there five hours before my flight, I had many areas to explore.

After walking for just half an hour, I was only just short of seeing half the airport and was pleased to rate it as one of the best in the world, on par with Singapore's Changi Airport. Then to my surprise, I found a shop offering foot reflexology and a spa. It's always amazing what you'll come upon when you take time to explore and greet the world with an open mind. In the hustle and bustle of the nine-to-five shuffle, most people miss a lot of what the world has to offer.

The menu of services included foot massage, shoulder massage, Thai massage, and aromatherapy. I inquired about the aromatherapy and thought it novel because it included a shower, which was exactly what I needed. For one hour, a lovely young Thai lady performed a much-needed, full-body, relaxing oil massage. This was followed by a refreshing shower, which combined with the massage left me feeling exhilarated and ready for the upcoming fourteen-hour flight.

I truly recommend making the most of every opportunity that greets us in our daily lives. Most people these days are in such a rush that they no doubt miss all the good things that are sitting right before their eyes, including the benefits of an oil massage at the airport while waiting for a flight.

My fourteen-hour flight from Bangkok to Los Angeles marked another break in my journey, with another overnight stay at an airport hotel in LA. But this time, I had to wake up very early for a 6:10 a.m. flight. Flying domestic in the United States used to be fun. It was very quick and efficient, but all of us must concede that the infamous events of September 11 affected domestic travel—for security reasons, of course. Prior to September 11, you could check in comfortably within one hour. These days, however, it's become a real chore.

My advice for any sort of travel is to check in really early. Give yourself two to three hours. If you have an early check-in between six and eight o'clock in the morning, then have a really, really early night the night before. You will need it, because these days, with self-service check-ins, you certainly do not want to be tired. You do not want to misplace any of your items, and you definitely do not want to get in the wrong line. Further, you want to be at your best to make the most of time that many people wish away—one wish that always comes true.

For instance, for the final sector of my journey from Los Angeles to Atlanta, I had to check in for my 6:10 a.m. flight. Therefore, I decided to leave my hotel room at half past three. The taxi to the airport got me to the United Airways check-in line before the ticketing counters opened. But there were at least sixty people already in line.

After the self-serve check-in process, I had to get in another line for boarding pass verifications. By the time I got to this queue, it had already grown to about one hundred people. While I was standing in line, I couldn't help but notice the many drawn-out, bored expressions on people's faces. These people must not have expected such delays, but instead of stare into space, I decided to stand in line and read. I was duly rested and ready for the delays that are a part of the flying process these days.

The final wait before I went to the departure gate was for our hand-luggage screening. This was yet another hundred-people-long line. So, with a sly smile on my face, I continued to read and enjoy the process of flying.

Even though I'm well versed with flying these days and can limit the personal dissatisfaction that may come with flying, it does not make me immune from everything. One of those many things that can go wrong with flying just so happened to occur to me when I landed in Atlanta.

Waiting at the baggage claim belt seemed to take an unnecessary amount of time. Then it occurred to me that my luggage had not arrived. I waited another ten minutes, but still no luggage. So I strolled over to the United Airways office to inquire. And sure enough, the lady told me that my luggage didn't make my flight in Los Angeles but would be arriving later that evening. She said the airline would deliver it to my hotel.

"Perfect" was my response. "At least I don't have to carry that luggage with me now."

After exchanging details, I was soon on my way to the Sheraton Gateway in Atlanta, where I would be for the next five days, attending the Find Your Why and Fly Main Event. It certainly helps give you peace of mind to believe that everything will work out in your favor, that all things are possible, and that, if great things can happen to other people, they certainly can happen to you. In the meantime, I like to follow one of Mahatma Gandhi's quotes, even in the smallest ways in my life: "Be the change you want to see in the world."

About the Author

Stephen Metcalfe is a geophysicist working offshore for the past fifteen years on research vessels, imaging the structures beneath the ocean floor for oil companies in pursuit of tomorrow's oil and gas fields. He has worked all over the world from Tasmania in Australia, throughout Southeast Asia, India, Africa, Brazil, Mexico, the United States, and Canada. Stephen currently works for BOS International Ltd., a company of Bergen Oilfield Services, Bergen, Norway. He lives in Perth, Western Australia, and has three lovely daughters: Namfon, Sharlene, and Jessica.

Stephen is determined to create a business for himself so that he has more time to share with and mentor his children. Stephen may be contacted through his blog at http://Business-Reviews-Online.com/BroINSIDER, his twitter page at http://twitter.com/stevemetcalfe, or by email: steve@Business-Reviews-Online.com.

With Freedom in Mind

Jatinder Singh Palaha

From the moment humans are conceived, amazing reactions take place. Cell division begins and continues until the baby's entire body is made. It's incredible to think that humans were once the size of a thumb inside their mothers' womb. From the beginning, we are constantly changing.

One of the first things to begin forming is the human brain. Once the brain forms, neuropathways are burned to record our experiences, which in turn shape our model of the world. In some cultures, surrounding the mother with a nice environment is considered good for the developing baby because people believe babies learn even while in the womb. A positive environment means positive effects on the newborn and vice versa. In a way, this is true for adults, too.

Scientists marvel at the human brain, which is by all accounts a very clever organ. Humans are considered highly intelligent because of their ability to learn in complex ways. The human body learns via the five senses of touch, smell, hearing, sight, and taste. Through these senses, we are bombarded with millions of pieces of information at any given moment. Some sources say that the human brain can cope consciously with only about seven pieces of information at a time, while the rest is processed by the subconscious mind. These experiences and neuropathways make it possible for us to learn and develop from a very young age.

So just imagine what happens to newborns as they enter this world. All those initial experiences are probably overwhelming. I'm sure I cried, but as I became more used to the experience, I probably calmed down. After the experience was over, I probably become familiar with it, storing it away somewhere in my brain for use later on.

Deceptive Perception

As we get older, our experiences continue to form us into a product of our conditioning. Learned experiences become the norm, and we run on autopilot, responding to our experiences with learned responses and behaviors. When we are in autopilot mode, we are under the false impression that things are happening *to* us, as opposed to the reality—that we are creating our experiences. If you become aware of the experience you just had and how you reacted or behaved in response, then you can empower yourself next time to choose consciously how to behave instead of just reacting. Things happen in life, but how you react to them and receive that information is something you can choose. You can choose to respond to life in a positive manner.

Think about it: Are your thoughts yours? Or are they influenced by society? Most of us do not see the world in its totality. Societal influences and our conditioning filter out parts of reality. If you know how you are influenced, you can become free. If you know the extent of your perception or the degree of your conditioning, you can see reality in its full glory.

We sometimes forget that our experience is never the same as someone else's; we may have similar experiences, but never exactly the same experiences. Even two people who experience similar things can and do react in quite different ways. Now, if someone else can react differently to something, then why can't you? Your perception can be a deceptive because it may not reflect what has actually happened. What you create in your mind is what you create in your mind. That creation may or may not be an accurate reflection of reality.

Once I saw a small waterfall and lake beneath a bridge. On one side, there were fish. It had been raining, so the waterfall was running faster than usual. I went to feed the fish some bread, but as I threw the bread, all the fish rushed to eat it, and most of them got caught in the waterfall and ended up on the other side of the lake. I felt sad at the time, as my inner voice said, "Oh no, the little fish have been separated from their parents, and it's all my fault." I never would have thought that by feeding them, I would separate the fish from their families. That wasn't my intention. I realized then that things often don't happen the way we intend. We have perceptions in our minds based on what we want to happen or what we think will happen, but when those things don't happen, we often realize the illusion we had been under.

To save myself from feeling so badly about things in the future, I would have to go into situations with no expectations about outcomes. Rather, I needed to train my mind to accept the things that happen and move on—a tough task, but possible. The fish appeared to make the adjustment. The next day, they all appeared as content as could be.

The Need for Change

We've all heard the expression that practice makes perfect. But what exactly are we practicing? The more we do something, the more comfortable we become. We form habits, and in some cases, we become professionals in whatever it is we practice regularly. Unfortunately, that can become a lot like playing the same old record over and over. It can get to the point where even thinking about changing the song can send shivers down our spines because what we are comfortable with is all we know. The unknown can be frightening. There's no question about that. But the unknown is nothing more than a perception of one possibility within a realm of endless possibility.

If that's the case, if anything can happen, why not aim to do something different or new every day? Maybe you don't want to. If that's your situation, then nothing will change in your life unless something external happens requiring you to make a change. You may be perfectly content doing what you're doing, but other factors can intrude. Perhaps no one is buying the widgets you enjoy making. Perhaps bad weather sets off a chain reaction that ultimately affects your life in dramatic ways. By trying something new every day, you prepare yourself for the unexpected and make yourself more versatile. Aim to become aware of what you are doing so that you can give yourself more choices and thus create new neuropathways. Doing something new or differently is always weird because we are not used to it; the neuropathways don't exist until we create them in our minds by doing new things.

A friend once said to me that he sees life as a stairway. When I asked what he meant, he said, "You have choices, right?"

"Right."

"And with choices we take action, and our actions have a reaction. So your action might take you up, and the reaction might push you down. Your choice sets a direction. Action has a reaction; hence, the motion is set once again in a certain direction. How many choices—how many actions and how many reactions—will take you up to ascension or down to dissension?" The step you're on is a result of your actions, and the choices you make will constantly set your direction.

We make choices and decisions every day based on some inner reason that stems from our experiences. Our decisions become so second nature that we forget why or how we do things. Much of our life is simply habitual. Sometimes we think we don't have a choice in what we do, but we always have choices. We just give priority to the things that seem more important at the moment. Choices are what got us to where we are now. However, because of habit, sometimes we make decisions that later we don't like, and then our perception can cause inner turmoil because we habitually see things a certain way, and the unexpected can break that illusion. Rather than see this as a chance to learn or see the world differently, many of us frustrate ourselves trying to force reality to fit our illusions.

Have you ever watched children at play and thought, "I wonder why they did that?" But perhaps we should be asking if the children made conscious choices to do certain things or did them simply to discover what would happen. Children will do pretty much anything and then learn from the experience. If they enjoy the experience, they will want to do it more. If they do not enjoy the experience, or get bored, they won't want to do it anymore. Most of us lose this sense of adventure and flexibility as we age and are conditioned by our experiences.

Sometimes we have to be "unreasonable" with the conditioning of our minds. Just because something did not work out does not mean it never will. That would be a generalization. When something doesn't work out, ask yourself what you could have done differently and in what other ways you could have approached the issue. One thing you might try is to look at the way others have done something, learn from their experiences, and apply them to yourself. Let your mind work on problems. That's its job and purpose. Trust it. In the end, it's the only thing you've got all to yourself. The thoughts inside your mind are yours. You put them there. Obviously, they can be influenced by others, and some thoughts can be planted in your mind by others. But your mind is yours, and at the end of the day, you should make sure you are the one who most influences your own thoughts and therefore your actions and your future. You always have a choice.

About the Author

Jatinder was born in the UK, the child of parents from the Indian state of Punjab (Hoshiarpur). As Jatinder grew up, he watched the hardships his father encountered: not knowing the language fluently coupled with the hard physical labor he endured so that Jatinder could have a decent education. Because of this, Jatinder wanted to do whatever he could to help his father. His father's wishes became reality when Jatinder graduated with a BSc in information systems and later went on to work with a Fortune 500 company.

Jatinder is a web designer who happens to have a passion for personal development. He has a partnership company, and one of his niches is working within the personal development industry, creating websites for life coaches, success coaches, and small businesses, exposing them to the masses so that they can actively work on making a difference in the lives of many. Jatinder is also a certified master practitioner of Neuro-Linguistic Programming (NLP). For more information, visit www.BigFanta.com or www. jatinderpalaha.com, or email jatinder@bigfanta.com or jt@ jatinderpalaha.com.